W9-CPC-751

"Treston presents here a new vision of religious education that is both pragmatic and pastoral. Catechists will appreciate his many suggestions for group activities."

Anne Marie Mongoven, O.P.
Santa Clara University

"What I like about this book is that it invites catechists to think globally. It challenges them to reflect on issues like creation spirituality, multi-culturalism and ecumenism. And yet it suggests numerous ways to teach the bible, Scripture, prayer, morality, and church in very practical ways. It will help veteran catechists enhance their skills, and it will introduce beginning catechists to a new and broad vision of their teaching role."

Gwen Costello
Editor, *Religion Teacher's Journal*

"*A New Vision of Religious Education* brings together unobtrusive scholarship, reflection on a wide range of religious issues, and a wealth of suggestions for action. It is an ideal book to peruse for creative, imaginative ways of teaching, and to keep on one's desk as a reference. I see it appealing to a broad spectrum of religious educators in many different settings."

Maria Harris
Author, *Teaching and Religious Imagination* and *Fashion Me a People*

"Kevin Treston has put together a resource book for religious educators that not only informs theoretically but is equally helpful practically. Perhaps the book's greatest contribution comes from exploring religious education within global and planetary implications."

Dr. Janaan Manternach & Dr. Carl J. Pfeifer
Authors, *Creative Catechist*

Kevin Treston

A NEW VISION OF

RELIGIOUS EDUCATION

Theory, History, Practice, and Spirituality
for DREs, Catechists, and Teachers

XXIII

TWENTY-THIRD PUBLICATIONS
Mystic, Connecticut 06355

Acknowledgments

I would like to express my sincere thanks to many people, especially to Kathryn for her encouragement and support in this project. In particular, I wish to thank the following people for their helpful advice and suggestions: Graeme Barry, Margaret Forde, Sister Gemma Moore, Tim Keating, Father Michael McClure, Tony Willmett, Beverley Smith, Brother Greg Palmer, David Boulton, Mike Mumphrys, Karyn O'Reilly, Beverley Tronc, and Gerard Sullivan.

Twenty-Third Publications
185 Willow Street
P.O. Box 180
Mystic CT 06355
(203) 536-2611
800-321-0411

ISBN 0-89622-558-5
Library of Congress Catalog Card Number 92-63178

Foreword

I can't imagine a more demanding or worthwhile vocation today than being a Christian religious educator! What a challenge to bring together the rich tradition of Christian faith with the lives of contemporary people, and to mediate between them in ways both *faithful* to the tradition and *life giving*. The challenge is heightened by the complexity, diversity, technology, and bureaucracy of our "modern" world. Indeed, Christian religious education, though never an easy ministry, has probably never been so demanding.

As in all eras before us, we need "new wineskins" for the task. That's where *A New Vision of Religious Education* comes in. The images that comprise its "new vision" are drawn from the communal memory of the Christian community, as well as from creative movements in the present. It draws from both memory and imagination; as such, it is a most "timely" contribution.

As Kevin Treston remembers and renews the tradition and builds with imagination on much hard-won wisdom, he focuses in particular upon "the teacher"—and fittingly so. Since the dawn of history, the key variable in every educational enterprise, that which most influences its measure of success, is the teacher.

Oh indeed, a fresh sign of hope in our time is renewed recognition that the success of religious education demands a partnership between "parish," "family," and "school." (I put all three in quotes because each must be redefined far beyond traditional boundaries and stereotypes.) Rather than depending on any one agency or person, Christian education calls for a quality "faith-life" in people's immediate relationships and base communities, and some ongoing access to "curriculum" that can support the life-long journey toward Christian conversion. In other words, "sharing our faith" is the responsibility of every Christian "worth his or her salt" (i.e. who take baptism seriously). And yet, having said as much, we must then remember that from the beginning of this faith tradition, we have recognized a unique and indispensable role for the teacher.

Daniel's apocalyptic angel of the end-time announces that those who teach others the ways of God's people will shine like the stars forever (Daniel 12:3). Jesus echoes this sentiment, saying that teachers of his way will be "great" in the Kingdom of God (Matthew 5:19). "Teacher" is the most frequent title used of Jesus himself in the New Testament, and his public work is described as "teaching" more than 150 times. According to Matthew, Jesus' last mandate to the disciples was "go teach" (28:19). In the first Christian communities, the *didaskalos* was recognized as a principal minister in a triad with apostles and prophets (1 Corinthians 12:28). *The Didache* (circa 100 C.E.) urges Christian communities to elect for themselves bishops and to treat them with the same respect that they already have for the teachers. And the teacher has continued in a crucial role throughout history; in fact, the fortunes of the church's faith education have risen and fallen with the quality of its teachers.

Effective religion teachers do not depend primarily on their professional expertise or their knowledge of content and methods, important as these may be. They depend most on their own appropriation of Christian faith as their personal vocation and call to holiness of life; this "owned" faith commitment must permeate their content and methods if their teaching is to be integral and effective. To repeat what I have written many times before, "the heart of religious education is the heart of the religious educator." It is the personal faith of educators when woven throughout their curriculum (content, method, and environment), their spirituality as teachers if you will, that most shapes what happens at the core of intentional faith education. Such integration and integrity, in turn, point to the need for wholistic and ongoing formation for our catechists and teachers.

That the spirituality and ongoing conversion of the teacher is the bedrock of religious education has always been true, but again this poses a particular challenge in our own time. For so long, Catholic education of all kinds was staffed predominantly by ordained or vowed religious, people who had received significant spiritual formation.

For example, in the American Catholic schools of 1963, 85% of all teachers and staff were clergy/religious and 15% were lay people. But twenty years later, the figures are almost exactly reversed with now 87% lay people staffing Catholic schools. The figure is probably even higher in parish religious education programs.

Rather than being "of little faith" and bemoaning this situation, we must take it as the work of the Holy Spirit in our time and place, but then redouble our efforts to attend to the spiritual nurture and ongoing faith development of our catechists and teachers.

Any resource for such wholistic formation should be welcomed as an asset, and Kevin Treston's *A New Vision of Religious Education* makes a mighty contribution. He lays out the pedagogical and theological foundations for the task, summarizes its central themes, and surveys a variety of teaching styles. Every chapter is structured to bring teachers into dialogue with the text, with their own praxis and faith, and with each other. It is this conversational dynamic, and how Treston has woven it throughout, that will enhance the personal formation of catechists and teachers. He dwells explicitly on spirituality in the last chapter, but the personal nurture of the teacher is also his goal in all the other chapters.

My hope is that this text will be widely used as "a conversation piece" for gatherings of catechists and teachers. "Old hands" who, like Kevin himself, have borne the heat of the day, will find blended together here much wisdom that may sound familiar but could be forgotten as memory fades. "Newcomers" will find here an excellent overview of what is best in the literature and field of religious education. But it will be the conversation this book can stimulate that will make the difference for both. I hope that *A New Vision of Religious Education* will be an occasion for the outpouring of God's Spirit when the old ones may "dream dreams" (again) and the young ones "see the vision" (Joel 2:28).

Thomas H. Groome
Professor of Theology and Religious Education at Boston College
Author, Sharing Faith *(HarperSanFrancisco, 1991)*

Dedication

To my parents, to Kathryn for her loving support,
and to all religious educators,
especially the Marist Brothers.

Contents

A NEW VISION OF RELIGIOUS EDUCATION

Introduction

One of my special childhood memories is of my mother sitting on my bed before I went to sleep, teaching me the catechism and overseeing evening prayers. My mother would ask me questions from the catechism and help me with the answers. Then I would say my prayers. In this tender way I was introduced to religion and to God. My mother was my first teacher of "the Way," the name the first Christians gave to the following of Christ.

This book is intended for all those who teach others about "the Way": catechists, religion teachers, adult educators, DREs, principals, and parents. Its underlying theme is the person and message of Jesus who is a new creation for our world. The context of the book is an exploration of religious education within an emerging global and planetary consciousness. I have sought to integrate theory and practice throughout.

Each of the twelve chapters contain—in addition to the development of the topic inself—Ways to Respond and Questions for Reflection and/or Discussion. The opening five chapters deal with broad areas of concern, and the following five apply these concerns to teaching five specific topics: the bible, prayer, the church, sacraments and sacramentality, and morality. The final two chapters encourage religious educators to 1) use "story" as an overall approach, no matter what the topic, 2) to continue to grow spiritually, especially through their religious education efforts and activities.

An extensive bibliography appears at the end of this book, which includes many of the works cited in the text. What makes this bibliography special is that it includes recommended resources from people who are actively involved in religious education as catechists, DREs, authors, and editors. They really *use* the resources they recommend and consider them invaluable in their religious education ministries.

For all these reasons, *A New Vision of Religious Education* is an ideal in-service training resource for new catechists and teachers. Veteran religious educators will benefit from it, too, especially from its global perspective. They will be reminded that there are many broad, global issues that now have an impact on those they teach, and these issues will also affect their content and teaching style.

My fervent wish is that this book will help all religion teachers to be more creative in their efforts. The good news of Jesus is an exciting challenge and ideally should reflect all the dynamism and vitality of the kingdom of God. My prayer is that *A New Vision of Religious Education* will be a helpful contribution to the communication of the beautiful story of God's love in Jesus.

Foundations of Christian Religious Education

One of my favorite Zen sayings is: "Don't just do something, stand there!" Busy religious educators can become so involved in the preparation and conduct of the lesson that they never seem to pause and "stand there." Teaching religion requires a great deal of energy and skill so catechists are easily absorbed into the dynamics of the lesson. When they "stand there," however, they are able to reflect on the whole enterprise of Christian religious education and situate each lesson within a total vision and context of communicating the gospel. I have chosen the following Zen story: "The Man and the Strawberry" to illustrate what I mean.

Once upon a time, a man was crossing a field. Suddenly a tiger appeared behind him. He fled across the field and tumbled over a cliff. As he was falling, he clutched a branch and hung on for dear life. Above him the tiger growled. He was about to drop down the small cliff and escape, when, to his horror, he saw another tiger waiting for him below. What could he do? At that moment, a rat poked his head out of the cliff and began to chew the fragile branch. The man looked around in desperation to save himself. Then he saw an overhanging strawberry branch with one ripe juicy strawberry. With his free

hand, he plucked the strawberry and ate it. How delicious was the strawberry!

This book invites catechists and teachers to step back from the "tigers" of everyday pressures to "pluck strawberries" by reflecting on an overall vision of Christian religious education.

When one engages in Christian religious education, there are certain dimensions or overall themes that need to be considered. I can think of many, and I list them here as a kind of "credo" for catechists. I suggest that if catechists are attentive to these elements, their efforts will be fruitful.

The First Is Love

Love is the giving of oneself to bring life to another. Teaching is sharing one's gifts to bring about new life in another. Love is a dynamic force in the whole universe to generate new life. When catechists and teachers love their students, they enter more fully into the divine mystery of God's love for us. The first letter of John expresses this extraordinary gift of love: "God is love and whoever remains in love, remains in God" (1 John 4:16).

The bottom line of Christian religious education is that God loves us and this love is not conditioned by our weakness or lack of fidelity. God's embrace is our first claim to fame. Isaiah images this love through the relationship between mother and child: "Can a woman forget her baby at the breast, feel no pity for the child she has borne? Even if these were to forget, I shall not forget you" (Isaiah 49:15).

Most of us are so accustomed to love being measured and portioned out that we struggle to appreciate God's love, or we find it difficult to make the leap in faith to believe in such a love. Perhaps we have been too hurt, or our love has been stunted. The challenge is for us to allow this kind of unconditional love into our consciousness. If we keep trying to let God's love transform us, then we will be able to respond more fully to loving relationships with those we teach.

Sometimes it's so hard to love our students. They can be uncooperative, rude, and scornful of our efforts. Remembering God's love will challenge us to go beyond the boundaries of our religion lessons. The climate of Christian religious education should reflect the presence of a God of compassion. Long after a religion class is over, the memory of care (or lack of it) will remain as a testimony to the quality of love experienced during the lesson. Most of us can recall teachers who were people of love or hate. We may have forgotten their names but we will never forget the kind of relationships we experienced with them.

Every religion lesson offers some image of God. A poorly prepared lesson taught with casual indifference may suggest that God is not really very important or worth the effort. An enthusiastic catechist conveys the impression that the gospel is alive and exciting. The witness of catechists to the integrity of the gospel challenges students to evaluate their own beliefs and values. In every lesson we should be revealing something more about the God of love.

Christ the New Creation

Jesus is the most dramatic expression of God's love. Jesus experienced a profound intimacy with God. The word *Abba* (papa or daddy) names the depth of this relationship. To call

God *Abba* is to liberate us from the burdens of our brokenness because it reveals a childlike trust in God's generous love.

Jesus is the new creation because he reveals a compassionate God who has affirmed our humanity through his own life: "He is the image of the unseen God, the firstborn of all creation, for in him were created all things in heaven and on earth" (Colossians 1:15-16).

The healing ministry of Jesus revealed God's desire for a more harmonious world. The kingdom of God presented people with exciting possibilities for a new creation in the world where true justice would reign with a restoration of right relationships. A new paradise would bloom if people accepted the radical propositions of Jesus. Jesus invites us to a way of responsible care for all God's creatures, especially the marginalized.

To engage in such unbounded care is to become vulnerable to the destructive powers of vested interests. The passion of Jesus is a poignant reminder of the bitter price to pay for affiliation with the underside of society.

By facing death, Jesus overturned the deepest fear in humankind. Death is integral to the transformation of creation. Death does have meaning within the context of new life and resurrection. The resurrection of Jesus is the promise and symbol of our own transformation. God raised up Jesus from the tomb to be a source of hope and a focus of reconciliation:

He is the beginning, the firstborn from the dead so that he should be supreme in every way; because God wanted all fullness to be found in him and through him to reconcile all things to him, everything in heaven and everything on earth, by making peace through his death on the cross (Colossians 1:18-20).

Christ is both redeemer and "reminder." He is redeemer because his life, death, and resurrection lead all creation to new life. He is "reminder" because he tells us who we are and who we might become. The *Abba* God becomes visible in the person of Jesus.

Jesus is the pivot of Christian religious education. He is the core of the Christian story: "For this is how God loved the world: he gave his only Son so that everyone who believes in God may not perish but may have eternal life" (John 3:15-16).

In the beginning the darkness of the world was dispelled by the light of God the creator (Genesis 1:3). The new creation was inaugurated by the coming of the Word of God, who brought light into the world: "The Word was the real light that gives light to everyone" (John 1:9).

Catechists and religion teachers need to reflect on the strength of their relationship with Jesus and the quality of Christology in their programs and schools.

Abundance of Life

Our own human experience is one of the beginning points for religious education. Jesus calls us to an abundance of life (John 10:10). The historical Jesus of Nazareth is the archetypal figure of what it means to be a human person. The followers of Jesus attempted to communicate to us his teachings, but also the power of his life, which had transformed theirs.

Human beings struggle with questions about ultimate meaning, their place in the universe, the significance of death, suffering, and religious beliefs. During the last 100 years, the extraordinary advances in human wisdom, especially in such fields as psychology, sociology, and anthropology, have brought us to a new level of consciousness about being human. While the contemporary movement in personal insights was a healthy corrective to the tyranny of corporate systems such as Nazism, Communism, and Fascism, the shadow side of personalism was the generation of the cult of individualism. The "I-me-mine" value sets great store on personal fulfillment to the detriment of communal values.

Today transpersonal psychology (which explores human behavior within the context of an interconnectedness with our total environment) and creation theology offer us theories and paths to reconnect us to our universe. Other theories of human experience, such as kinesthetic psychology (dealing with an awareness of wider sensory phenomena), help us to appreciate extraordinary possibilities for our creativity and imagination.

I suggest that humankind is on the verge of a great leap in our knowledge and appreciation of the psyche and the spirit of being human in a partnership with our universe. Research on the functions of left and right brain thinking has helped us to integrate both rational and symbolic approaches to education. The implications of the movement toward wholeness are profound for religious education. The divisions and classifications of our culture fragment the way we perceive reality. We desperately need a unified vision of our world.

Catechists might well ask if their teaching is really an invitation to a fullness of life. The history of Christian religious education provides many somber reminders of how easily the incarnation of Jesus with all its implications for celebrating an abundance of life has been betrayed by legalism, dualism (in which body and spirit are separated), and scorn for bodily pleasure. A zest for life and faith that Jesus can transform us surely are signs that Jesus is an animating power in our lives.

Revelation

Revelation is what God communicates to us. God yearns to share gracious life with us, drawing us more deeply into the embrace of love. Revelation helps us enter more fully into the mystery of God's presence in the universe and be more aware of our call to image God. God communicates with us in many different ways. Every living creature expresses God's revelation in some diverse way.

For a Christian, there are five dimensions of revelation.

•Ourselves: We learn about God by reflecting on the seasons of our life journeys, on our feelings, our relationships with others in the world, and our search for fulfillment.

•Our World: By attending to the world and our culture, we can observe God's Spirit moving through all creation. God is revealed through the events of each day. For people of faith, the whole of the universe is alive with the presence of God.

•The Bible: The bible is the story of God acting in human history. By meditating on the bible, we discover the unfolding revelation of God through the saga of the Hebrew people and the culmination of revelation in the advent of Jesus the Christ.

•The Church: The teachings and life of the Christian community throughout two thousand years help us experience God's revelation. The church is the community founded by Jesus to proclaim the good news of the kingdom of God, to live out the gospel values in community and to work for a more harmonious world.

•Jesus: The climax of God's revelation is the person of Jesus. He is the "finger of God," light for the world, the face of God's love.

All five dimensions of Christian revelation should be evident in a comprehensive religion program. During the period from the Middle Ages until the mid-twentieth century, the teaching church was considered the key dimension of revelation. The contemporary church is sensitive to keeping a more healthy balance between all five dimensions of revelation so as to be more faithful to God's ongoing communication with us.

Culture and the Kingdom

God's revelation is always to people in some specific era of human history within a particular cultural environment. Many of our assumptions and symbols about religious education within a particular context are not necessarily valid for people in other parts of the world. The ministry of Jesus was experienced in the culture of first-century Palestine. The Christian church rapidly became Greek in its philosophy and theology, and Roman in its law. The structures of the church were modeled on the bureaucracy of the Roman Empire. The dynamic symbol of the kingdom of God became identified with the visible Christian church. After the sixth century, Christianity and European culture were virtually synonymous. Christian religious education over the centuries became an extension of European culture as well as teaching about Jesus.

Since the 1960s we have become more aware that we are a multi-cultural people. Catechists today are challenged to interpret the Christian message to multi-cultural groups. They cannot assume that Anglo-Saxon middle class white values are acceptable norms. Neither can they adopt an alien or hostile stance toward our culture by dismissing it as secular or materialistic without exploring possible meeting points. The gospel is to be announced within every cultural situation, and catechists must listen to the many cries of our culture. By attending to the culture and sharing the joys and pain of their students, they become companions along the way.

Religious education is rather messy because it engages the chaos of living with its ups and downs, mortgages, boredom, surprise at a birthday party, birth of a child, beginning high school, and watching the first gray hair appear. Therefore, questions such as the following are useful to consider: What are the life concerns of those I am teaching? Where are possible meeting points between the gospel and the values in their cultural environment? What are some cultural signs of the times that reflect an unfolding revelation of God to them?

Inculturation is the term we use to describe the interaction between the gospel and culture. During the 1970s, the church became more aware of the need to continually reinterpret its message in a pluralism of cultural forms and symbols. Christianity is gradually moving away from a kind of European cultural imperialism to an acknowledgment that each cultural group shapes the good news of the gospel according to its symbols and myths.

Invitation to Faith

Christian religious education is an invitation to allow one's faith to be deepened. Faith is a gift from God. One cannot acquire faith simply by reading about it. Faith is a response to God's loving wish to be more present in our lives. Christian faith implies a movement from ourselves as the central focus to compassionate service of others. Religious faith is a leap of trust in God whose face is often obscured. Faith is not simply an assent to a series of doctrines, but rather a way of life that reflects deeply held values.

Faith cannot be imposed. Indoctrination is a contradiction of the very essence of religious education as an invitation to grow in faith. In answer to the two disciples of John who asked Jesus about his lifestyle, Jesus said: "Come and see" (John 1:38). Yet, freedom to choose in faith has had a very tenuous history in the Christian story. After the tumult of the Reformation, during which the authority of the church seemed to be eroded, Catholic leaders tended to view religious freedom as a dangerous luxury. After the sixteenth century, the Catholic Church was a church under siege. Absolute adherence was demanded and enforced.

The Second Vatican Council restored the more traditional understanding of faith as a free gift from God that must be accepted freely. It is not static, but rather a living thing that motivates believers to carry the gospel message into all their daily activities.

A Kingdom Vision

Christian religious education is the sharing of the dream of Jesus to make present the kingdom of God. Conversion to the kingdom means that we will follow a path of reconciliation with God, with others, and with our world. To be a kingdom person is to imagine and live a radical alternative way of relating and being. It is to experience God as *Abba*, to have "shalom" as our motto. Every dream has its price, however. The trauma of Calvary was the terrible cost extracted for Jesus' kingdom dream. Yet he went bravely toward his death and thus transformed our existence by overcoming the bondage of death through resurrection. By becoming brothers and sisters of Jesus, we rejoice at our adoption as sons and daughters of God.

The kingdom message is one of hope and encouragement. The climate of hope should permeate the whole enterprise of religious education. The affirmation of the gospel message challenges the pessimism of our culture. While religious educators do not deny the prevalence of evil and the anguish of a groaning world, a kingdom vision holds fast to a message of possibilities and human treasures that are discovered with surprise and delight (Matthew 13:44).

Creation

During the latter part of the twentieth century, we have been rediscovering the interrelatedness of all things in the universe. Almost too late, we have begun to listen to Earth as a silent partner of the universe and to acknowledge that we are integral to all creation, not superior to it. The theme of creation is a yeast for religious education. God's spoken word of love creates the world. The creator God continues the divine fertility by breathing into life woman and man. The garden symbol situates humankind within a paradise of harmony and cooperation. Humankind, as epitomized by Adam and Eve, is designated co-creator with God for the ongoing evolution of the world.

Sin is a choice to move away from this harmony and wholeness. Sin is alienation from the essence of being a fully human person. Sin, as described in the opening chapters of Genesis, is both communal and individual. However, God's faithful love brings together the earth and heavens in a rainbow covenant between God, us, and Earth: "When I gather the clouds over the earth and the bow appears in the clouds, I shall recall the covenant between myself, you and every living creature, in a word all living things" (Genesis 9:14-15).

Our current ecological crisis calls us to return to the primal tradition of the original covenant between God, us, and Earth. Reverence toward the universe implies an attitude of humble stewardship, rather than of arrogant domination. Creation theology and spirituality provide a wholistic framework for our relationship with our world. Throughout the centuries, Christians have so emphasized redemption that they tended to focus on salvation in the next world rather than attend creatively to the building up of this world. Redemption and creation are complementary, not opposites, in our experiences with God. Christian religious education leads us to a creative participation in the evolution of God's great dream for the whole of the universe, not simply the well being of humankind.

Listening

Christian religious experience is a Word experience. The spoken Word of God moves through the world with the power to create and change those who are open to its energy. Isaiah describes how the creative Word of God, the *dabhar*, brings God's will to fruitfulness: "For, as the rain and snow come down from the sky and do not return before having watered the earth, fertilizing it and making it germinate to provide seed for the sower and food to eat, so it is with the word that goes from my mouth: it will not return to me unfulfilled or before having carried out my good pleasure and having achieved what it was sent to do" (Isaiah 55:10-11).

Religious education continues the cycle of God's wisdom and challenges us to respond. The parable of the sower and the seed (Mark 4:1-9) describes six possible responses for those who encounter the Word of God. A person may ignore the word, symbolized by the birds who carry away the seeds. Another may accept the word for a while but soon gives it up, symbolized by the seed that grows and is withered. Others may live by the word for some time before opting out of discipleship, symbolized by the thorn bushes that suffocate the growing seed. There are also those people who rejoice at the word and experience God's power in their lives as symbolized by the 30-, 60-, and 100-fold harvest.

A "banking" theory of religious education implies that the teacher is the fount of knowledge and the students are empty vessels to be filled with information. A dialogue theory of religious education proposes that religious educators acknowledge the gifts and wisdom of all participants. By listening and attending to the stories of students, teachers ground their approaches in the reality of lived experiences as well as becoming learners themselves. Faith is a groping toward light rather than a triumphant march along a road of certain truth. In each age of emerging consciousness, the Christian credo has to be reinterpreted for people with new symbols and language to communicate the divine mysteries. Religious educators should regularly ask themselves: What did I learn from my students today? Do I take their comments and responses seriously? Do they perceive me as a good listener? Am I really a catalyst for the Word of God?

Ethics and Justice

All sound education influences the way we act and modifies our value system. Christian religious education seeks to transform values in society so that people are enabled to live more fully as human beings who are created in the image of God. The growing gap between rich and poor, the proliferation of nuclear weapons, the rape of Earth affront God's plan for a harmonious universe. Over one-quarter of the world's population lives in poverty. Half the world's scientists are employed in war-associated industries. Since 1945, there have been 845 atomic or nuclear explosions by the United States alone.

Christian religious education can never be a detached academic study of the phenomenon of religion. The way of Jesus as described by the gospel writers is a lifestyle of service, love, and reconciliation. The teaching church throughout the centuries has struggled to integrate the expanding horizons of knowledge with its moral imperatives. The Beatitudes provide a values framework for Christian morality. A religion teacher is faced with such questions as: How possible is the Christian lifestyle for people of this culture? How is an ethical stance communicated without the danger of over-moralizing? How should people judge right and wrong in a pluralist society?

Principles of Education

Effective Christian religious education has to be consistent with sound contemporary educational theory. Attention to research on learning will surely affect the processes that are employed in religion lessons. Many a well-intentioned lesson has faltered, not for want of sound theology, but because basic management skills have been disregarded or principles of education have been ignored.

Educational theory in the latter part of the 20th century shifted the learning focus from teacher-centered to student-centered learning. Students became much more active participants in the learning process. Educational theorists like Peters, Dewey, Freire, and Kohlberg have shaped the style of contemporary education.

Many religious educators today like Thomas Groome, Gabriel Moran, and Maria Harris are challenging catechists to employ sound educational principles. Until very recently, Christian religious education was a child of theology, rather than of education. Consequently it was shaped by a model of communicating a series of dogmatic beliefs. Catechists might want to evaluate their teaching by responding to such questions as: Do my lessons incorporate sound principles of education? Do I try to use basic management skills? Are my lessons creative? Are my students really learning through my lessons?

Components of Religion

Christianity, in common with all the great religions of the world, has several dimensions. Although theorists of the phenomenon of religion propose different classifications for these dimensions, there seems to be considerable consensus on the following components of religion:

•Beliefs: Religious belief is what is professed by the group and held sacred. For example, in the Christian religion belief would be Christian doctrines.

•Stories and Texts: Stories are the sacred narratives that comprise the religious traditions of a group. The text is the written word or scriptures of the group. For example, in the Christian tradition the stories tell the journey of people moving from primordial time to historical time as the chosen people of Yahweh. The Jesus event and early church story constitute the second part of the Christian bible.

•Ethics: Ethics is religious reasoning that offers a rationale for the behavior and morality of a group. The Ten Commandments and the Beatitudes indicate not only a code of behavior but an attitude toward relationships within the Christian tradition.

•Rituals: Rituals are the sequence of sacred actions that link the worlds of the ordinary and the sacred. In the Christian religion, liturgy and sacramentals are examples of sacred action.

•Social System: This is the visible structure that provides an institutional form for the religion. The church is the social system in Christianity.

•Experience: The experience dimension of religion is the way in which people enter into a relationship with the divine and express their devotion. Examples from the Christian tradition are ecstasy, mysticism, charismatic prayer, the rosary, and biblical meditation.

Christian religious education needs to be situated within diverse religious traditions. Religion addresses the great question: What does it mean to live, given the fact that one day I will die? In Western society, religion, especially in its institutional expressions, is being questioned about its relevance. Many young people wonder if religion has any meaning in our world. Freud considered religion a sign of stunted psychological development, while Jung believed that the most important questions in the latter phase of the life journey were ultimately religious ones. Karl Marx attacked religion as an opiate that dulled people from social analysis and action.

An awareness of the various components of the phenomenon of religion suggests the need for a comprehensive curriculum to incorporate its different dimensions. Evaluation of many religious education curricula indicates that some components of religion have been so emphasized that other dimensions are impoverished. For example, if morality or religious practice become the main focus, ritual or scripture may be neglected. The study of religions has helped Christian religious educators to appreciate their own tradition among the rich heritage of many others.

A Lifetime Journey

The theme of journey is a core motif in the Judeo-Christian saga. We are travelers along the way, negotiating the passages and seasons of life. Religious education is a life-long enterprise. In faith we believe that God is inviting us to grow in love at every stage of the journey.

The concept of "birth-to-death" or "cradle-to-grave" religious education means that opportunities to expand one's consciousness about the religious tradition are provided throughout every phase of one's life. In practice this means that there should be provision for children, youth, *and adults* in religious education.

The early Christian church directed its catechetical energies toward adults. In this century the church has tended to limit religious education to children. During the last decade, however, adult faith education has gradually been developed and restored as a vital partner to child-centered religious education. However, child-centered religious education still takes center stage for an allocation of resources.

Religious Readiness

By religious readiness we mean the ability to comprehend religious concepts. Any experienced catechist is well aware that children in the same class are at very different levels of understanding religious concepts. Children in the intermediate grades, for example, while able to conceptualize religious dogma and to engage in abstract thinking, do not do so uniformly. Levels of religious readiness are determined by such factors as age, intelligence, family religious socialization, and the instructional environment. The concept of religious readiness is an important one because it affects what we teach, how we teach, and the expectations we have about the outcome of our teaching.

I have vivid memories of my feelings of despair-laughter-disbelief when correcting sixth-grade religion papers in the "old days" and reading extraordinary interpretations of the words Annunciation, Magi, and Immaculate Conception. Clearly, the religious readiness of the students was far removed from the curriculum I was asked to teach. If teachers ignore religious readiness and attempt to communicate content that is beyond the level of the group, they must expect disinterest, apathy, and even hostility. The whole issue of religious readiness is compounded by a post-Christian social environment. I was startled recently when an 18-year-old student in a religion class asked me quite sincerely if Jesus had written the bible!

Family Religious Education

In the Judaeo-Christian tradition of religious education, the family has always been regarded as the principal agent for religious socialization. Christians inherited the great injunction in the book of Deuteronomy: "You must love Yahweh your God with all your heart, with all your soul, with all your strength. Let the words I enjoin on you today stay in your heart. You shall tell them to your children, and keep on telling them" (Deuteronomy 6:5-7).

Through the ordinary (and extraordinary) events of family life: the laughter and tears, celebrating and grieving, loving and hurting, family members can discover God. The Vatican II document on the laity describes the family as "the domestic sanctuary of the church." Family religious education is authentic because it is firmly located within the most significant influence for socialization. Family life can be a very powerful nurturer of the values of love and care, but today it is under severe threat. Fragmentation of the family unit is tearing apart the very fabric of our society. The church needs to affirm family life in every possible way and religious educators should work toward full family involvement in parish programs. Such programs must include families in every situation: single-parent families, multi-cultural families, poor families, etc.

Teaching as Ministry

Christian religious education is ecclesial because its mandate is situated within the mission of the church to teach (Matthew 28:19). Jesus founded a community to be proclaimers of the gospel. A Christian community is a witness to the message of the kingdom of God as well as its announcer. Religious education becomes a lived reality for those who experience the celebration of a vital Christian community through its worship, witness, and service. Prayer and worship reflect the beliefs of the community. The ministry of teaching is named by Paul as one of the special ministries of the early church (1 Corinthians 12:28). Christian religious educators are conscious that they teach in the name of the church and have the responsibility for communicating the Christian way with integrity and fidelity.

The magisterium of the church is that body of teaching which reflects the distillation of doctrine and practices. Religion teachers in the Christian tradition have inherited a set body of doctrinal teachings. They cannot pick and choose which aspects of Christianity they will teach or ignore. Yet there are inherent tensions in being engaged in the ministry of teaching because at times the official church stance may be at variance with kingdom values, for example the subordinate role of women in church. However, Christian religious educators are accountable to the wider church community and exercise their ministry by fidelity to the basic credo of the church.

Trinity

The Trinity is the heart of Christian revelation. The mystery of the Trinity expresses our most profound belief in the meaning of being a person. We are created in the image of a God of relationships. Our sexuality reflects the dynamic life of God which is always unfolding in a capacity to love and to be vulnerable. The father/mother images of God reveal that we are sons and daughters of God, brothers and sisters of the Son, Jesus, and empowered by the generativity of the Spirit.

Because Christian religious education is basically trinitarian, it is necessarily relational. Catechists should therefore strive to establish a good rapport with their students and to build a climate of trust and love. When the atmosphere of their classes is open and respectful, students feel free to explore their religious questions without pressure. They can let go of fears that inhibit honest questions. Learning is enhanced in an environment of trust and affirmation. When teachers refuse to tolerate dissenting opinions, they evoke feelings of hostility or apathy. The model of Trinity encourages them to discover the gifts of the Spirit within the group and to share the gospel message through teaching, sharing, reconciliation, and challenge.

Religious Literacy

An important goal of Christian religious education is to develop religious literacy so that students are competent to express themselves in religious language. Many adult Catholics lack confidence to discuss and share their thoughts and feelings on religious issues. Otherwise, very articulate professional people will often fall silent in a group meeting about prayer or spirituality.

In moving away from the set catechism formula approach into the language of the new theology since Vatican II, some people became confused by "new" words like ministry, spirituality, evangelization, liberation theology, praxis, and mysticism. These are examples of key concepts, yet their meaning is far from clear in the minds of many Catholics.

Religious education empowers participants to think religiously and to acquire skills to analyze religious questions. In a culture dominated by scientific assumptions about the nature of experience, it is imperative that our young people are able to critique the philosophical framework of our society and propose a vision for our world based on a religious appreciation of all human beings.

Evaluation

The general movement toward more accountability in education at state and local levels challenges religious educators as well. Within the Catholic community, the emergence of lay catechists has raised many questions about commitment, competence, and suitability for the task. Post-Vatican II theology is more fluid and relational and hence appears to be more tenuous for those accustomed to clear and definitive statements on dogma.

Evaluation is a general term for a consideration of the purposes of religious education in a parish or school. It examines the role of religious education within the Christian community, how it affects people, how the curriculum may be developed, and what new options are possible for greater effectiveness.

Sound evaluation procedures suggest that there is an appropriate reporting process to students and parents. Students must also be involved in reviewing the effectiveness of their religious education programs. Care should be exercised by teachers in avoiding the impression that evaluation implies a judgment on the personal faith life of the students.

Imagination

The role of imagination in religious education is to open our consciousness to new horizons of being and God imaging. The gift of imagination is like a magic carpet that carries us to a place of creative possibilities. When Jesus was beginning his parable teaching, he introduced his stories with the invitation to listen and imagine (Mark 4:2). Stories and parables take us to places beyond our conventional barriers and stereotypes.

Though we might be immobilized by a sense of powerlessness and inevitability, imagination encourages us to ask: Why not? Provocative teaching is an echo of the radical attempt of Jesus to break through the encased religious boundaries that had trapped many of the ordinary people in first-century Palestine.

The gospel injunction to become a child for the kingdom (Matthew 18:3) is a conversion to wonder, awe, and creativity. Sound religious education integrates right and left brain learning producing a healthy mix of the rational and the aesthetic. An over-emphasis on a doctrinal approach is like trying to trap the mystery of God within the confines of language. While religious experiences should have a rational framework, they should also invite us into possibilities in our relationship with God.

Transformation

Victor Turner, one of the leading anthropologists of this century, proposed three basic stages in the process of change for cultural transformation (see his book *The Ritual Process* in Suggested Resources):

1) Separation: a group moves away from a set cultural position

2) Liminality: the group moves through a threshold stage of searching, evaluating, and experimentation

3) Aggregation: the group incorporates the experience of passing through the threshold stage and assumes another position which has been enriched because of the trauma of its passage time.

With varying degrees of intensity, the Catholic church and other Christian churches have been moving through a stage of liminality. Vatican II was a step into another religious place for many Catholics. The stage of liminality is still very much in evidence as the community moves away from a patriarchal and authoritarian style of leadership to one based on collaboration and sharing. Hopefully the pain and excitement of this stage will lead the Catholic community to an enriched appreciation of its mission to transform the world with kingdom values.

Christian religious education is often at the center of the storm of liminality because the character of religious education is at the cutting edge of the new consciousness. Catechists can easily become scapegoats for the frustrations of those who wish to return to the "golden age" of the church. Such people see nothing positive emerging from the liminality stage.

Catechumenate

The restoration of the catechumenate in 1973 (*Rite of Christian Initiation of Adults*) offered religious educators a primal model for catechesis (based on the first five centuries of Christianity when the catechumenate flourished). The four stages of the catechumenate: inquiry, instruction, initiation into the community, and the deepening of conversion, are four possible movements for any catechetical approach to religious education.

Inquiry encourages interested people to search, question, and discover. Instruction communicates the Christian story which is celebrated in prayer and worship. Initiation is the step of commitment. Enlightenment or deepening the experience provides the initiated with the opportunity to become familiar with Christian rituals, lifestyle, and community. The four movements of the catechumenate remind us of the need to synthesize the doctrinal, liturgical, apostolic, and communal dimensions of catechesis within a faith community.

Ecumenism

Christian religious education is ecumenical because it intends to raise humankind to a new awareness about God's manifestation of love. In our present age, there is a yearning to discover our common roots with our brothers and sisters throughout the world. Confronted with serious threats to our very existence from the depletion of Earth's resources, famine, nuclear weapons, and exploding populations, many religious groups are joining together in a common search for ultimate meaning by cooperation and reconciliation.

In a special way, the demolition of the Berlin Wall represented humanity's hope for peace and unity. Hopefully the tragic era of sectarianism has passed. Ecumenism does not mean a denial of our own particular religious traditions but an affirmation of the universal search for the divine presence from various perspectives. Each religious tradition: Islam, Hinduism, Judaism, Buddhism, Christianity, is a deep well drawing water from the underground river of God's revelation.

Mysticism

Mysticism is the bringing together of all things to a wholistic vision and experience of God's oneness. In the mystical journey, we let go of various blocks and securities and open ourselves to allow the God of the heart to become the axis of our being. The "image of God" is the turning point of our consciousness.

Many Christians associate mystics with religious fanatics. But we are all mystics, or at least should be. Mystics see things as whole rather than in parts. Mysticism removes us from the chains of legalism and formalism which stultify growth and change. As we journey inward to the source of our being, we are given a more expansive picture of God's dynamic love transforming the world. Religious educators are mystics when they see beyond the immediate to the essence of their enterprise. Mystics are "heart" people because they lead us to the core of things rather than allow us to be distracted by marginal issues. They speak of experiencing total union with God where "God as other passes away" (Eckhart).

Feminist Influences

The emerging feminist consciousness is having a profound influence on the scope and direction of theology. Women theologians such as Rosemary Ruether and Elisabeth Schüssler Fiorenza are beginning to restore balance to a theology that was previously written from a male perspective. Our society has been impoverished by patriarchy which sets male norms as the reference point of our social structures and values. The Christian churches, reflecting the sexual patterns of the cultural environment, have engaged in institutionalized discrimination against women through their structures and ministry. The radical vision of Jesus toward women was quickly lost in the primal Christian communities.

Today we hope to return to the tradition of complementary partnership between men and women and allow all the gifts of the community to be gathered and shared. If religious education is to be wholistic, it will challenge exclusive male images of God and the delegation of women to inferior roles in church life. Christian religious education will find inspiration for God imaging in the literature of Wisdom where the Spirit of God is described as feminine. Certainly, Mary, the mother of Jesus, is a gospel model for all oppressed women (Luke 1:46-55).

Spirituality

Spirituality is a faith journey of discovery toward wholeness. Through our spirituality, we are responding to the invitation of a loving God to enter a deeper communion with God and our world. Those who are engaged in the pursuit of spirituality are actively involved in the creation of a better world. During the Middle Ages, a dichotomy between theology and spirituality developed and both areas of Christian life were impoverished by this split. There was a corresponding split between spirituality and religious education. A spirituality for religious education gives substance to the exploration and communication of God's presence in our world. Religious education without spirituality is an academic activity without a heart. Spirituality without religious education is a quest without direction or roots.

Liberation

The Gospel of Luke records the beginning of the public ministry of Jesus in the synagogue of Nazareth. Jesus opened the scroll and read from Isaiah: "The Spirit of the Lord is upon me...to bring the good news to the afflicted...to proclaim liberty to captives, sight to the blind, to let the oppressed go free, to proclaim a year of favor from the Lord" (Luke 4:18-19).

This text quoting Isaiah might well be a basic charter for religious educators. Teachers cannot tolerate any form of coercion and unjust use of power. Power is the way we influence people. As an ideal, the Christian stance toward power is to set people free to live more responsibly and fully. The only significant temptations for Jesus as recorded in the gospels relate to his use of power. The history of the church is a rather somber reminder of the prevalence of the misuse of power.

The Exodus story is a model for catechists to journey from slavery to freedom. When we engage in struggles for freedom, we usually become more free within ourselves as well.

Conclusion

These dimensions of religious education provide catechists and teachers with a perspective of how diverse elements interact. A unifying vision of religious education enables them to see links between such activities as organizing school liturgies, providing resources, supporting discouraged parents, and planning community service activities. What unites all of these endeavors is faith in God's love for us as expressed through Jesus.

Ways to Respond

Reflect on each of the twenty-seven dimensions of religious education discussed in this chapter. Do this by making a chart with three columns. List the twenty-seven themes in the first column. In the second column list the way these themes are part of your present classes. In the third column list ways that you might add this dimension to what you are now teaching.

Questions for Reflection and/or Discussion

•Which of the dimensions described in this chapter do you consider "essential"? Why?

•Are there dimensions you can think of not mentioned here? What are they?

•How did you feel after reading this first chapter? Excited? Discouraged? Optimistic? Why do you feel as you do?

•The author explains that his ultimate purpose is to help catechists and teachers experience the reality that "Jesus calls us to an abundance of life." Why do you think this is so important?

•How might you share the information in this book with those you teach?

Notes

Creation Theology
and Religious Education

One of the most urgent tasks in contemporary religious education is the fashioning and communication of a comprehensive spirituality and theology of creation. Creation theology has emerged as a response to the cries of an exhausted earth and the search for a sustainable economy. Almost every day the media reports stories of threats to our ecosystem: ozone layer depletion, the greenhouse effect, salinity, relentless march of the deserts, and the burning of rainforests. After centuries of hibernation, churches are now joining the wider community in a chorus of protest calling for concerted action. Scientists warn that our generation is possibly the last that will have the opportunity to make radical changes in our relationships with Earth, and the church is finally taking heed.

Christians and Earth

Christians have always been ambivalent about their relationship with Earth. The first Christians inherited a Jewish tradition that was unsure if absolute loyalty to Yahweh could be reconciled with an earth partnership. Their neighbors engaged in fertility rites and pantheism, which they scorned. And yet, the land was a special symbol of their covenant with Yahweh.

Jesus affirmed creation by his presence on Earth. He used earthy images in his teaching and much of his public ministry was spent moving from place to place in the countryside. The mustard seed is a symbol of the kingdom of God (Matthew 13:31). Jesus spoke of the beauty of creation: "Think how the flowers grow; they never have to spin or weave, yet, I assure you, not even Solomon in all his royal robes was clothed like one of them" (Luke 12:27). Bread and wine, made from wheat and grapes, are the two basic symbols of the presence of Jesus in the Christian community.

In the first decade after the death and resurrection of Jesus, many Christians believed that the second coming of Christ was imminent and thus saw no reason to become involved in the world, except as a means to individual salvation. Throughout the 2000 years of Christian history, this theme has persisted. The earth has been viewed as transient, a testing ground for heaven. The real business of life was to avoid sin and save one's soul. Yet, Christian theology has celebrated nature through its symbols of fire, salt, water, candles, wind, and oil. Earth is a sacrament of God, and nature is a book of revelation about divine imagination. The monastic tradition deeply influenced Christian spirituality in two divergent ways. The "flight-from the world" movement tended to reinforce a view that salvation could not be found in the world, but only in the refuge of a monastery. However, the farms and estates of the monasteries grew prosperous because of loving care for nature. Celtic, Franciscan, and Benedictine spiritualities are grounded in a celebration of creation.

The dualistic heresies separated body and soul. Heretical groups such as the Gnostics, Manicheans, Albigensians, and Jansenists eroded the oneness of creation and the reality of the incarnation. These groups taught that the body is only an inferior vessel for the soul, which is God's spirit. The denigration of the body, especially our sexuality, included a contempt for the world as of no real consequence. Although dualism has been rife in Christian spirituality, the creation tradition is gradually surfacing again as a response to the ecological crisis. Creation theology, like liberation theology, is entering the mainstream of theological thought in our contemporary church.

What Is Creation Theology?

Creation theology is an exploration of the relationships between God, us, and our world. God is love. Love generates life. Our whole planet and cosmos are expressions of the artistic generativity of God as creator. The first covenant between God and Earth is symbolized by a rainbow (Genesis 9). We are to be stewards of the land, not dominators. Yahweh reminds the people that they are strangers and guests in the land (Leviticus 25:23). The image of the paradise garden evokes our deep yearnings for a harmonious Earth and thus we are to be sensitive gardeners, not plunderers.

Unfortunately, the injunction to "fill the earth and subdue it" (Genesis 1:28) has been the justification for the rape of the earth. Recent biblical studies have helped us recognize that the command of Yahweh was rather to care for Earth as responsible stewards.

God's creation of our universe is at least fifteen billion years old. Humankind is about four million years old. Until recently, theology addressed only the story of humankind as if all other life in the universe was some kind of adjunct. The problem of "homocentrism," the exclusive focus on humankind, marginalizes all of creation and distorts the true meaning of men and women as beings within a living universe. To know ourselves, we need to appreciate our identity within the whole universe. Christ is savior for all creation (Colossians 1:15), not simply for one group living on one planet. Modern theories of science describe the marvelous interconnectedness of all living things.

The first peoples, for example, the native people in North America, the Aboriginal people in Australia, and the tribal people in South Africa, celebrated the integrity of all creation. European colonists came to the lands as arrogant masters rather than humble learners. Only now are we beginning to appreciate the wisdom of our first peoples who knew about the essential oneness of all living things. Christians are expanding their Christology to include Christ's saving love to all creation. The death of Jesus is not only the agony of every homicide, suicide, or genocide but also the anguish of biocide (death of species) and geocide (death of a planet). Creation theology situates the story of humankind within the intricate web of relationships between all of God's creation.

Why Is It Emerging Now?

Like all theologies, creation theology is not new, though it certainly has become more significant today. The most obvious reason is the crisis in ecology. Toward the close of the twentieth century, we have become more conscious that humankind faces an environmental catastrophe of unimaginable proportions. This generation probably has the final responsibility of trying to reverse what is happening to Earth. Earth is tired and crying out for us to care about it and be prudent in the use of its resources. The simplistic view of Earth as a bottomless well of resources has been thoroughly discredited.

The church has a serious responsibility for using its authority and resources to renew the earth as a bio-spiritual planet. Thomas Berry, one of the foremost spokespersons for Earth today, has repeatedly warned that if this is not attended to immediately, an overwhelming amount of damage will be done, and an immense number of living species will be irrevocably lost for all future generations. The environment question is essentially a religious question about how we are to value God's creation. If God's revelation in creation is diminished, so is our own identity.

The prospect of a nuclear holocaust has hung like a sword over fragile international relations since World War II. The world now possesses the power to destroy itself. The disasters of Chernobal, Bhopal, and the Challenger explosion were terrible reminders that there is no such thing as foolproof technology.

Features of Creation Theology

•Right Relationships with Earth

The foundation of creation theology is the quest for right relationships between God, us, and Earth. Because there is every prospect of space colonies being established in our generation, the scope of creation theology has to include the whole universe. The first photo from the moon beamed back to us in 1969 heightened our awareness of the beauty and uniqueness of our planet. Russell Schweickart, one of the four who traveled on that historic journey to the moon, later wrote: "You realize that on that small spot, that little blue and white thing, is everything that means anything to you—all of history and music and poetry and art and death and birth and love, tears, joy, games, all of it on that little spot out there."

Through creation theology, we celebrate the divine artistry of the creator and watch in wonderment the unfolding of a beautiful world. Earth is a sacrament of God's presence and providence. If we develop a sense of awe and mystery toward Earth, we will learn to reverence its secrets, colors, and seasons of life and death. Earth is not to be used irresponsibly. We are stewards and partners with it and humankind will be held accountable for care of it. Earth is a meticulous bookkeeper who will finally insist that we pay our debts. Those who abuse it denigrate their own humanity. Those who reverence it become more attuned to the possibilities of human creativity.

•Sabbath

The Sabbath has a special significance in creation theology because on the seventh day God orchestrated the symphony of creation through contemplation. The western world has been so locked into the "six day working God" that it has overlooked the climax of creation in the Sabbath. In Sabbath we pause to experience the *berakah* or blessings for the fertility and generativity of creation. As God the artist danced to the music of God's creativity on the Sabbath, so we, too, are invited to wonder and imagine. The Sabbath is a day to rekindle the fires of creativity.

Through the *kairos* of the Sabbath, we are empowered to become prophets of imagination because we listen to divine possibilities through the tapestry of creation. Sabbath challenges us not to be seduced by voices of compulsive activity or prophets of economic doom. Through faith, we know that the divine imagination is not limited to our petty horizons. We must dare to be different. The prophets of the bible, especially Jesus, transported us to places far beyond the acceptable limits of religious boundaries.

•Imagination for Justice

Prophetic imagination encourages Christians to critique social, political, and economic systems. Together, we must make a commitment to work toward a sustainable economy that is congruent with responsible stewardship. Issues such as foreign debt, which is crippling third world peoples, have to be honestly faced. How practical is it for conservationists to insist that fringe dwellers in desert lands cease chopping down trees and halt the march of deserts when they need the wood for fires during the freezing nights? We may decry the rape of the Amazon forests, but how does Brazil pay its enormous foreign debt?

The vast majority of the world's population lives in capitalist or Marxist systems that reduce people to economic units in an industrial machine. There simply has to be an alternative social and economic system that enables people to eat and live with dignity. During the next century, there will be increasing migration of young populations from third world countries to first world countries to fill the labor market. Such a migration implies a world climate of multi-culturalism and multi-racism which enables the new peoples to live in genuine social communities.

As religious, social, and national barriers disappear, are we prepared to live in a new style of world community? Creation theology challenges us to make courageous decisions to work toward a new world order that is more in harmony with the paradise story.

•The Importance of Work

Throughout history, work has generally been viewed as an essential but unfortunate activity. Christians inherited at least three traditions of work. The Greek attitude is expressed by Plato in *The Republic:* Work is the lot of slaves, the lower class, and certainly not the business of the ruling classes and people of intelligence.

A literal reading of the Genesis account of the Fall would suggest that work is a punishment for the first sin. Later in church history, people such as the Jansenists proposed that work is a necessary element of our sinful humanity. By enduring suffering in this world and having to work hard, we will never be tempted to become attached to earthly things. Grinding labor makes us want the joys of heaven much more ardently.

Over the last few centuries, our economic systems have been dominated by the symbol of the machine. Many workers have become alienated from work and separated from the fruits of their labors. Wages have replaced the intrinsic meaning of work. How many workers really only live for the hours after work, weekends, and holidays?

Creation theology explores the meaning of work as co-creation. Through work we continue the ongoing creation of work in God's world. The various employments: bus drivers, homemakers, teachers, factory workers, shop assistants, management personnel, all contribute to making a better world. Creation work enhances our world. Such work utilizes the resources of the world and our gifts for the welfare of humankind. Our diverse gifts as workers can lead us to new harmony if these gifts are shared in a cooperative community.

•Women and Men in Partnership

Creation theology is also concerned with right relationships between men and women in partnership. We must discover the gifts of both men and women through cooperative ventures for the healing of our planet. When one sex is relegated to an inferior status, the other sex is corrupted. Over thousands of years so much creativity has been lost because of the inferior status accorded to women.

Patriarchy, an affront to the human community, is based on a domination model of relationships. Unfortunately, it has been religiously endorsed by male imaging of God. As long as we are locked into male images of God, we limit our appreciation of God's very nature. At the best, we can only know half of God when our images are exclusively male.

The first Christians struggled to preserve the radical vision of Jesus. He did not limit discipleship to males, though this was the custom of other rabbis. The first evangelizer in the Gospel of John is a Samaritan and a woman. Matthew's Jewish community must have found it difficult to accept that the proclaimers of the resurrection were women; yet women were not permitted to study the Torah.

A popular Jewish prayer chanted by men was one of thanksgiving for not being slave, servant, or woman. Church historians estimate that within 40 years after the death of Jesus, Christian communities had reverted to the practice of regarding women as part of the property owned by the male head of the household. The most influential theologian of the Western church, Thomas Aquinas, provided another theological rationale for patriarchy when he described women as "misbegotten" males.

If we Christians are committed to right relationships in the order of God's creation, we need to allow the underside of history to be told and give space for the silent voices of our history to be heard. Our communities will be enriched by the incorporation of the wisdom of the feminine into the mainstream of our consciousness. Unless women are part of collaborative ministry, the church will have difficulty in its credibility when it speaks about justice and human dignity.

Science and Religion

Scientists and theologians should be companions in their respective fields of inquiry. Both seek to unlock the mysteries of our place in the universe. Since the seventeenth century, science and religion have been antagonists. However, the ecological crisis of the twentieth century has drawn them together. Since the middle of the twentieth century, scientific theories have become wholistic, flexible, and global rather than quantifiable, logical, and specific. A new scientific vision is dawning in which the essential oneness of the universe is being understood. The scientific revolution of the last 300 years lost its way when we knew all about the parts but could not see the whole. We are now beginning to appreciate that science is one of God's special revelations to us, provided we utilize its wisdom.

Descartes gave a philosophical rationale for the perception of nature as being "out there" by his separation of mind and matter. This comment by Francis Bacon, regarded as the father of modern science is revealing: "Nature is to be tortured until it yields up its secrets." Newtonian physics explained the world as a kind of giant clock that faithfully followed scientific laws. Modern science is less certain about fixed laws and emphasizes a life force within the universe that generates energy toward the ongoing evolution of the world. Recent scientific theories of chaos are very attuned to the mystery of death and resurrection.

This development of real dialogue between religion and science is a hopeful reversal of a growing trend: the church talking to itself. Christ cannot be just a doctrinal Christ but is a cosmic Christ for all creation (Colossians 1:15). The identification of Christianity with European cultural norms left Christianity groping in its power to transform diverse cultures. Growing world consciousness is now evidenced by the ecumenical dialogue between the great religious traditions of Islam, Buddhism, Hinduism, Judaism, Taoism, and Christianity. We are searching for the *Atman*, the God beyond all the various divine images. We recognize that God's revelation is lessened if we lose even one of the scriptures or wisdom of any religious faith.

Conclusion

Christian religious education is expanding its horizons to include ecological religious education. We are awakening to the music of the universe and celebrating the sacraments of fire, wind, and water that speak to us about our oneness with Earth. The urgency of the environmental crisis warns religious educators that the task must be addressed immediately. The growing interest in mysticism suggests that we long to return to the core of our being within creation. Mysticism often surfaces in times of loss of identity and meaning. When our symbols and myths disintegrate, we are moved to recover our original story. Mysticism gathers our differences into a new mandala of God's love.

Ways to Respond

The following suggested activities will help you to focus more deeply on some of the principles of creation theology. Do these alone, with a group of catechists, or with older students and adults.

• Collect stories from various religions and cultures on the origins of creation. What is your favorite creation story?

• Find a nature place near your home and visit this place several times each year. Note the changes in nature during the seasons.

• Encourage your parish to celebrate a feast of creation.

• Compose an Earth book and record sayings and poems about Earth, for example: "The frog does not drink up the pond in which he lives" (Indian proverb), or "Walk lightly upon Earth" (Lao Tsu).

• Invite Native American speakers to share with those you teach their affinity with Earth.

• Plant a tree or shrub. Enjoy its growth.

• Compose a prayer service with the theme: "Earth, Our Mother."

• Pray this prayer of Francis of Assisi with those you teach:

Be praised, my Lord, for our sister Earth who cares for and sustains us and bears fruits of many kinds, colorful flowers, and grass.

Questions for Reflection and/or Discussion

• Have you personally become more aware of creation theology over the years? In what ways?

• How has this new awareness influenced your religion classes?

• In what ways do your textbook, curriculum materials, or other resources develop the themes discussed in this chapter?

• The author calls this a time of loss of identity and meaning, especially for Earth. He says that mysticism surfaces at such times. What do you think he means?

• Have you presently noticed that our religious symbols and myths are disintegrating? Is this true for those you teach? Why or why not?

Notes

The History of Religious Education

Throughout its two thousand years, the Christian community has shown flexibility in its various approaches to initiating people into the community and leading them to know Jesus and his teachings. The following brief survey of the history of religious education describes some of the church's main movements over the centuries. By looking at them carefully we can gain the perspective we need to go forward into the future in appropriate ways.

New Testament Era

The Gospels, Acts, and the Epistles indicate that the catechetical styles of the early Christian teachers were modeled closely on those of Jewish religious groups. In the long Hebrew tradition of religious education, there was great emphasis on memorizing stories and prayers as well as celebrating God's action in liturgical ceremonies. During the Bar/Bat Mitzvah ceremony, the young boy or girl was required to recite passages from the Hebrew Scriptures. Jesus would have studied the scrolls and chanted the psalms in prayer as any other Jewish boy did. The first significant conflict within the church community, that between the Jewish Christians and the Gentile converts, was largely settled by 60 C.E. Many of the Pharisaic missionaries from

Palestine, especially from the Jewish church, insisted on circumcision as a necessary condition of initiation into the Christian community. Such missionaries were firmly resisted by Paul.

The Council of Jerusalem in 49 C.E. was a watershed in that it moved the young church away from the dominant Jewish model for religious formation. The Christian message to the Jewish people emphasized Jesus as the expected Messiah. The Torah of Moses had been supplanted by the new Torah of Jesus the Lord. For the Gentiles, Jesus was preached as savior, redeemer, and transformer of all creation. As the Gentile converts became more numerous, the religious education activity of the Christian community assumed more characteristics of Greek and Roman cultures.

There were four main expressions of catechesis in the early church: 1) the proclamation (*kerygma*), 2) instruction of the people (*didache*), 3) participation in the Christian community through fellowship and worship (*koinonia*), 4) service to the community, especially the poor (*diakonia*).

As the churches began to be more firmly established toward the close of the first century, there emerged a greater need for concrete pastoral structures. Such structures evolved during the second century.

The Early Church 100-500

During these centuries religious instruction was directed toward adults, not children. The catechumenate was developed to provide a comprehensive formation in the Christian way. Many variations of the specific format of the catechumenate evolved in different localities, but there were three essential elements common to all.

1. Candidates for admission to the catechumenate were required to demonstrate that they were prepared to make a commitment to Jesus and accept a radical change in their lives according to the demands of Christian discipleship.

2. Formation of Christians-to-be was the task of the whole community. Often the instruction was conducted by laity, especially by relatives and friends of the catechumen.

3. Liturgical participation played a significant role in the candidate's formation. Initiation to the sacraments was a gradual process that received careful scrutiny by church elders.

Documents such as the *Didache* (late first century) and the *Apostolic Tradition* of Hippolytus (end of the second century) provide us with valuable details of the initiation process.

By the close of the third century, the catechumenate was much more structured. During the first stage, the candidates were admitted on the recommendation of friends or relatives, and the prospective Christians had to give evidence of serious intent. Before admission to the actual catechumenate, candidates were instructed in the basic truths of the faith. After admission to the catechumenate, the person experienced a comprehensive formation (over three years on average) and participated in the liturgy. Catechetical schools were established to train an increasing number of catechists who were needed for catechumenate instruction. The culmination of the formation process was the reception of baptism at the Easter Vigil.

Thus in the first Christian churches, there was a close correlation between liturgy and catechesis. After baptism, the new Christians spent time consolidating their faith commitment. This fourth phase of the catechumenate was called the "mystagogical" period.

After the time of Constantine, the church was permitted legal existence and soon became the official religion of the Roman Empire. The catechumenate began to decline in influence during the fifth and sixth centuries. Large numbers of people were becoming Christians, many with no inclination to make a radical commitment to Christ, but rather to be integrated into the acceptable social strata of Roman Empire. Infant baptism became the norm for entry into the Christian community. The church sought to preserve a preparation time for all Christians through the development of the lenten period before Easter, but the brevity of the time and the lack of clear goals about Lent reduced its effectiveness. Large numbers of barbarians were "converted" in tribal or military groups, making adequate preparation for commitment impossible.

As Christianity became socially respectable, the dynamic message of the kingdom of God was dulled by the imperatives of accommodation. Small groups of Christians fled to the deserts and hills to follow Jesus in an emerging monastic tradition.

To sum up, Christian religious education during the first five centuries contained these features:

•Adults, not children, were the focus of all catechetical efforts.

•The initiation period into the Christian faith was generally comprehensive and rigorous.

•The initiation period was a time of fasting, prayer, good works, and learning the truths of the Christian faith.

•Liturgy and sacramental preparation and practice were an integral part of the formation process.

•The community and parents were responsible for initiating children into the Christian faith.

•Christian centers of learning developed in cities such as Antioch and Alexandria.

Christian apologists and scholars like Origen, Clement, Cyril, Jerome, Augustine, Basil, and Gregory formulated Christian doctrine within a Greek and Roman cultural context. Two of Augustine's books, *First Catechetical Instruction* and *The Christian Teacher*, greatly influenced the direction of Christian education during the period of the rise of the monastic schools and the emergence of the medieval universities.

The Middle Ages

The most powerful influence in Christian education during the medieval period was the cultural milieu which was impregnated with religious meaning and symbols. Cathedrals, mystery plays, feast days, liturgy, devotions, art, language forms, all taught about the Christian faith. The cycle of life was lived within the seasons of the church year and the sacraments. Although Christianity was often reduced to a magical folk religion which exhibited a shadow side of savagery and barbarism, the whole fabric of the Middle Ages was essentially religious.

The consolidation of the clergy as a cultic group separate from the laity tended to reduce the liturgy to something performed by priests for passive congregations. The educational power of the liturgy was minimized by this lack of participation, and education for ministry was almost exclusively a clerical enterprise.

The sacrament of individual penance became widespread in the Roman church after the eleventh century, and the *Confessional Booklet* became a source of instruction for the laity. Monasteries and some small rural schools did try to provide rudimentary religious education for some children. Regular instruction included the saying of the Lord's Prayer and the Hail Mary, and learning the Decalogue and moral precepts. The rise of universities stimulated developments in theology and philosophy.

The synthesizing genius of Thomas Aquinas exhibited the best qualities of medieval education. However, his writings stressed the rational and cognitive. Faith was viewed as an assent to a series of doctrines. The eminence of Aquinas left a heritage of emphasizing the rational in religious education, often at the expense of Christian living and the salvation story.

Reformation Period to the Nineteenth Century

The religious upheavals of the sixteenth century gave great impetus to religious education. There was a movement away from the medieval view of children as "young adults" to children as young people. In the heat and fury of the religious conflicts, both Protestant and Catholics sought to consolidate their positions by propagating their beliefs about the most effective ways to educate. In 1529 Martin Luther published the first catechism. One edition was for pastors and catechists; another was for children. The invention of printing in the fifteenth century provided an accessible vehicle for the proliferation of ideas.

The Lutheran catechism was quickly followed by a Catholic one, or rather a whole series of catechisms. The catechisms of Canisius and Bellarmine and the Roman Catechism all forged a "catechism" tradition in Catholic education which has persisted well into the twentieth century. Indeed the catechism approach has been revived with the Universal Catechism promulgated in 1992.

The reformation catechisms shifted the accent of narrative, scripture, and Christian living, which characterized early church instructional writings, to concise summaries of church doctrines. The Roman Catechism, for example, contained these sections: Creed, Sacraments, and an explanation of the Lord's Prayer. The first Catholic catechisms were written for pastors, not for children. Later, when children's catechisms were produced, they tended to be modified versions of adult catechisms with scant regard for levels of readiness.

The Council of Trent (1537-1565) legislated the systematic instruction of adults and children. The catechism instructions that evolved after Trent focused on memorization of texts without a necessity of comprehension. Religious educators such as Fenelon, La Salle, the Jesuits, and Comenius continued to train teachers in religious education and to adapt religious instruction to a child's level.

With the rise of popular education in France, the German states, and England, the state and church struggled for control of popular education. Gradually the state gained the ascendancy over the church. The church in turn set up a parallel system staffed largely by religious congregations. Battle lines were drawn between church and state over who would teach religion and by what methods.

The Twentieth Century

By the beginning of the twentieth century, it was increasingly obvious that the catechism method of teaching religion was less and less effective or appropriate. The catechism belonged to an era when the prevailing culture was Christian and Catholics could and did live within a subculture of Catholicism. The de-Christianization of the masses in traditional Catholic countries—in spite of heroic attempts to transmit a Christian education through the catechism—provided evidence that this method simply would no longer work. The incorporation of psychology into education and the liturgical revival were other factors in modifying the catechism style of religious instruction.

At the beginning of the twentieth century, catechetical reforms, especially centered in Munich and Vienna, focused more on how children learn than on the text itself. The catechetical congress in Vienna in 1912 encouraged starting with a child's experience and working back to the catechism text. The catechetical conference at Munich in 1928 encouraged religion teachers to draw from the best pedagogical methods known and apply these to teaching religion.

Bible history studies were beginning to give the catechism a more scriptural orientation. In Europe and the United States, new editions of the catechism minimized the use of abstract language. The dominant model of religious education was associated with schooling and thus children were considered the focus of catechetical activity. Even the words "religious education" and "catechesis" became linked to what happened in a Catholic school or Sunday school class. However, after hundreds of years of a fairly static approach to religious education, dramatic changes were about to occur.

Between the middle of the twentieth century until now, Christian religious education has undergone a series of rapid transformations. Kerygmatic catechesis was the first of these movements.

Kerygmatic Catechesis

During the 1950s the catechetical scene was stirred by the infusion of kerygmatic catechesis, which emphasized the joy of the good news of salvation with Jesus at its center. The kerygmatic movement was rooted in biblical and liturgical revival. In one sense the church was rediscovering the intimate relationships between liturgy, the Word of God, and catechesis.

However, within ten years there was growing disquiet about the kerygmatic movement and doubt that it was *the* panacea for religious education. Kerygmatic catechesis was biblical at heart, but gave too little attention to the human situation. People might well ask about the relevance of the terms "salvation history," "Paschal mystery," and "covenant stories," if they have nothing to eat or are imprisoned without trial by ruthless dictators. Dehumanizing social situations cried out for religious instruction that addressed the pain of oppression.

The new phase in religious education, the anthropological movement, was clearly in evidence by the early 1970s.

Life-Centered Education

The life-centered movement in religious education took the real situations of people as its starting point. This phase was influenced by the growing popularity of psychology and the social sciences, as well as the growing gap between rich and poor in the world. A rediscovery of the dimensions of revelation that concerned the human condition gave a theological rationale to the life approach.

Biblical studies produced fresh insights into the cultural mores of Jesus in first-century Palestine. Terms such as: "exploration," "journey," "experience," "values," and "relationships" became standard language for catechetical texts and literature. Within the Catholic Church, the new emerging churches in Africa, South America, and Asia grew more articulate about catechesis within their own cultures.

The life-centered movement did not replace the insights of the kerygmatic phase but complemented it by its emphasis on the here and now. God's Word is revealed in our world, in our time, within our cultures. No sooner had the life-centered approach become established than it was being critically evaluated. There was always the danger that such a movement could become so personalist in its orientation that humankind—not God—would become the center of revelation. The cult of individualism could easily permeate the anthropological era of religious education. The way was opening for the next step in catechesis by turning the gospel searchlight on the structures of society to enhance authentic human values.

Political Religious Education

The catechetical conference at Medellin in South America (1969) proposed that catechesis should seek to assist human society to interpret its situation in the light of the gospel. Political religious education arose out of a cry for liberation and had its theoretical rationale in liberation theology. This movement in catechesis during the 1970s corresponded to the new wave of awareness in the church about social justice. How can the eucharist be celebrated by the community if the people have no bread?

Political religious education was a catechesis of social action. One of the concerns about this trend in education was the possibility that the

sense of transcendence and mystery would be diminished. Questions were raised, too, about the affinity of political religious education with Marxism. The wonder of the incarnation might be reduced to another ideology of revolution.

However, the political phase in the story of religious education has left an enduring heritage by incorporating a social justice dimension firmly within its theories and practices. The proclamation of the kingdom of God is here and now as well as hereafter. Questions raised about society evoked other questions about the social influences in faith development. And so the socialization phase of religious education surfaced.

Socialization and Religious Education

The socialization phase of religious education might be described as that movement which emphasized the significance of the Christian community in faith development. During the late 1970s increasing attention was given to the key place of family, parish renewal, small prayer groups, family religious education, and the climate of the Catholic school in providing an affirmative environment for catechesis.

The socialization phase drew its inspiration from religious education models in the early church and research that examined the critical role of a religious culture in faith formation. The shadow side of religious socialization is indoctrination and sectarian ghettos. However, in the face of a dominant secular society, religious educators rightly sought support and formation groups to facilitate faith growth.

Social Science

The social science movement in religious education originated from an educational context. It considered all the factors relevant to any learning experience and sought to maximize the effects of variables that influence learning. Some relevant variables that could have an impact on religious education are classroom atmosphere, the time of day or night, the professional expertise of the teacher, the physical environment for learning, the levels of readiness among learners, and the commitment of the teacher.

The social science movement started from the context of learning variables rather than theology, and hence to some of its critics seemed to be a secular version of the more traditional approaches to religious education.

Shared Praxis

The Shared Praxis approach is a style of teaching in five movements, which has been popularized by Thomas Groome. During the early 1980s the Shared Praxis approach was very popular, possibly because the five movements synthesized key insights from the previous twenty years of theory to a workable way of teaching religion. The five movements in the process are:

1. the students identify an action related to the topic for study
2. reflection on the action
3. the Story and vision of the Christian community are presented
4. interaction between the Christian Story and the individual stories of the students
5. reflection on the interactions and possibilities for future action and change.

The Shared Praxis approach has obvious value for developing a reflective style within the catechetical process. Its obvious limitation is its assumption that the members of the group are committed to the Christian faith, although Groome does recognize that people are at different faith levels.

Ecological Religious Education

The growing consciousness about the ecological crisis provoked Christian religious educators during the late 1980s to evaluate their programs from the perspective of creation theology.

Ecological religious education explores the kinds of conversations between people within the context of a world made holy and whole by a loving creator. Men and women were first formed within the environment of a harmonious garden. Yet humankind is faced with shrinking resources of a fragile Earth and dehumanizing technology. Ecological religious education opens women and men to paths of creative partnerships with Earth and with each other, utterly rejecting a subject/object way of viewing relationships. This phase of Christian religious education is rediscovering its primal roots in the first covenant of Noah which bonded God, people, and Earth in a solemn pledge of mutuality.

Catechetical Directories

In the 1970s, a series of catechetical directories were published that represented the church's attempts to understand and express catechetics based on the momentous implications of Vatican II.

These directories attempted to find effective ways of communicating the good news of Jesus in the modern world. The idea of a directory had been proposed before the Council, but the pastoral thrust of the Council and its dynamic theology gave impetus to this movement. The six "Study Weeks" organized by Hofinger influenced the scope and direction of the directories. The *General Catechetical Directory* was published in 1971. Three other Roman documents had important implications for catechetics. These documents were: *Directory for Masses with Children* (1974, updated in 1993), *Evangelization in the Modern World* (1975), and *Catechesis in our Time* (1979).

In the English-speaking world, the most comprehensive catechetical directory was produced in the U.S. in 1979 after extensive consultation. *Sharing the Light of Faith: National Catechetical Directory for Catholics of the United States* was a milestone in setting directions in Christian religious education.

Further Movements

Many other phases in the Christian religious education story are surfacing today. Feminist religious education is telling the underside of religious education and beginning to rectify the imbalance of theories written and directed by men. Only now are women theologians emerging in the church community to contribute to catechetical and religious education forums.

Ecumenical religious education has developed from the dialogue between Christians and the particular needs of religious education in public schools. It intends to further the study of religion in ecumenical settings.

Other significant trends in contemporary religious education include: an integration of spirituality with religious education, family religious education, aesthetics and religious education, imagination and religious education, and cluster religious education.

A New Catechism

In December 1992, a new catechism, *The Catechism of the Catholic Church*, was officially proclaimed by the pope as a "statement of the faith of the church and of official Catholic doctrine." The catechism intends to provide guidelines for ethical questions arising from complex political and social situations. It is divided into four sections: Part 1: The Creed; Part 2: Sacramental practice; Part 3: Moral teaching; Part 4: Christian prayer. The catechism has the potential to provide a unifying focus for Catholic catechesis. However, the rapidly changing theological landscape, influenced by such theologies as feminist, creation, liberation, and universal, will challenge those who wish to limit the unfolding revelation of God's wisdom by setting the text of the catechism in stone.

Conclusion

The story of Christian religious education illustrates its rich diversity and flexibility as it has tried to be faithful in its mission to "teach all nations." When we reflect on the courage, innovation, and faith of teachers throughout history, we are challenged to continue the search for effective ways of sharing the faith tradition by drawing from the wisdom of the past and imagining the future.

Ways to Respond

•Recall your own experiences in religious education. Identify the various approaches and name the phases that have affected you most profoundly.

•As a catechist or teacher, you need to be aware of the strengths and limits of each movement in the history of religious education. Make a list of the major movements, including: Catechumenate, Catechism, Kerygma, Life Experience, Shared Praxis, Ecology, Feminist, and Religious Studies. Beside each describe its strengths and/or limits, and reflect on ways that you might incorporate each into your teaching.

Questions for Reflection and/or Discussion

•Which is (was) your favorite phase in the evolution of Christian religious education? Why?

•Which phases have you personally experienced? How have they affected your teaching?

•Do you tend to think of religious education as flexible or inflexible? Why?

•Have you experienced religious education as something that offers you "rich diversity?" Why do you think this is so?

•In what practical ways might you begin drawing from the "wisdom of the past" in your teaching?

•In what ways can you begin "imagining the future" with those you teach or with co-workers?

Notes

Chapter 4

The Language
of Religious Education

"What's in a name?" asked Shakespeare in *Romeo and Juliet*. Religious Educators might well ask the same question about the multitude of terms used to describe their teaching activity. Many words are used to describe this enterprise. The following list of descriptions appears in writings about religious education: Christian doctrine, religious education, evangelization, catechetics, Sunday school, CCD, indoctrination, religious studies, adult religious education, Christian living, a study of religion, and religious instruction.

What do these words mean? Are there any real differences among them? Far from being a theoretical question, I suggest that the issue of clarifying language is one of the most fundamental questions to be addressed today. Specifying our religious education activity enables us to know what we are doing. For example, if catechists are teaching a course on religious studies, then they know that they are teaching about the *phenomena* of religion and not participating in a catechetical activity. Students will also be clear on what is happening lest they feel that they are being brainwashed or trapped by an imposed religious faith. In reality, however, a group of students may move easily from a study of a religious ritual to a

prayer service involving the ritual without intrusion. Let's look together at some of the terms presently in use.

Religious Studies, or Interfaith Religious Education

Religious studies is the study of the phenomena of religion. The teacher seeks to present the religious topic with objectivity and impartiality. Buddhism, Judaism, Hinduism, Islam, and Christianity are examined as important influences in the human story for enlightenment and the search for ultimate meaning. Each country has its own native religions as an object of study. The intention of teaching religious studies is not to convince students about the superiority of one particular faith over the others, but rather to discover the wisdoms of each religious tradition and to nurture the values of tolerance and respect.

Religious studies may be part of a school curriculum, especially in schools where there is a wide range of religious beliefs among students. Religious studies may also be studied in parochial schools. Care should be taken, however, to ensure that a comparative approach does not denigrate any religious faith. One difficulty with the religious studies approach is the question of communicating the meaning of a religious tradition when the teacher is outside the tradition itself. However, in an ecumenical climate, the study of religions has much to commend it.

Evangelization

Evangelization refers to the proclamation of the gospel. It influences people to hear the gospel and to be open to God's word. It is the preaching of the gospel. Jesus commissioned his disciples to go out and announce the good news of salvation to all. Evangelization is an essential element in the mission of the church. Mark's Gospel states: "Jesus went into Galilee. There he proclaimed the gospel from God saying: 'The time is fulfilled, and the kingdom of God is close at hand. Repent, and believe the gospel.'" (Mark 1:14-15). Evangelization is usually directed to people who are without Christian faith.

Catechesis

Catechesis follows evangelization. Catechesis is concerned with the development of the Christian faith among believers. It is a dialogue between believers. The word "catechesis" is derived from a Greek word meaning "echo" because after the second century catechesis was linked to the act of giving oral instruction to intending believers in the catechumenate. Catechesis seeks to foster faith, not just through learning doctrines, but through the religious socialization of the Christian community. Catechesis is an activity for believers and assumes that participants have chosen to be present or at least are willingly present and are people of faith. Liturgy and engagement in good works are integral to catechesis.

Religious Education

Religious education describes a relationship between religion and education. Religion is concerned with humankind's encounter with the divine, and it helps people discover answers to such questions as: What does life mean? Why is there suffering? and Who is God? Education is the endeavor to acquire knowledge, skills, and values for the enhancement of human wisdom. Education is a process of drawing out inherent gifts within the students as well as the transmission of knowledge, values, and skills. Since the 19th century, education has been closely linked with schooling, but obviously it is much broader than any one school system.

Religious education is the effort to know and experience the world of religion. It does not mean leading a child or adult to a faith commitment, but it may contribute to a position of faith affiliation. Religious education is a meeting point between religion and education, and implies a conversation between learning and the whole experience of the phenomenon of religion. Sound religious education has the following features:

• It is ongoing. It is not merely the transmission of knowledge.

• It implies a dialogue between teacher and students.

• Its content embraces the wisdoms of world religions.

• Its styles reflect the educational philosophy of the particular religion teacher.

• Social sciences, theology, and scripture have a particular relevance to it.

At first sight, it may seem that catechesis and religious education have few common elements. While in theory this may be true, all sound catechesis should include a sympathetic study of world religions, especially in acknowledgment of God's mysterious revelation through a diversity of traditions. The area of purpose or intent would be the point of parting of the ways between religious education and catechetics.

Indoctrination

This term describes a style of religious teaching that does not permit deviation from the party line and an official position. Indoctrination is intolerant of freedom of choice. No critical thought is permitted and religious development is channeled into prescribed boundaries. Indoctrination cultivates a hostile view toward other groups as threats to its ideology. Truth is what the teacher says is true. Indoctrination is contrary to the spirit of Jesus who invited people into a free choice situation: "Come and see" (John 1:39).

Adult Religious Education

Adult religious education is faith education for adults on the life journey. Because adult education focuses on adults, it needs to be faithful to principles of adult learning. Adults bring to each learning situation a wealth of faith and life experiences and expect some opportunity for dialogue and sharing of insights as partners in learning. Relevance is a basic principle for adult faith education. Busy adults have little time or energy for engaging in esoteric pursuits of remote academic questions. The term "life-long" religious education might be more helpful than adult religious education because it suggests a gradual evolution of learning passages rather than a clear differentiation between child and adult learning.

Christian Doctrine

This activity relates to the learning of dogma. Christian doctrine concentrates on the acquisition of knowledge of doctrines. It is an enterprise of the mind rather than the heart. The term "Christian instruction" is similar to Christian doctrine and emphasizes a cognitive approach to learning about a particular faith tradition.

For many years, the whole enterprise of teaching religion in parishes was referred to as CCD. This title came from the Confraternity of Christian Doctrine, an organization that developed four centuries ago in Milan, Italy. Its goal was to create "a strong, zealous lay apostolate working for the light of faith and the glory of God." Through it, people in parishes were trained to offer religious education to all children and youth not enrolled in Catholic schools. Nowhere was this movement more effectively organized than in the U.S., especially from 1930 to 1950. It led to the development of parish and diocesan catechist training programs and emphasized the call of lay Christians to proclaim the gospel.

Teaching doctrine was the focused goal of the Confraternity and its members. As we saw in the chapter on the history of religious education, the emphasis is broader today. In most parishes, religion lessons combine elements of evangelization and catechesis and doctrine is considered one of *many* components of the faith. Though a national organization of the Confraternity of Christian Doctrine no longer exists, the term CCD has come to stand for all religion classes. Diocesan and parish leaders today refer to parish-based religion programs as religious education, Christian education, or Christian formation, but old habits die hard and people continue to refer to them as CCD.

Christian Living

"Christian Living" was a popular name for Christian religious education during the 1970s. The term focused on the experiential dimension of Christian religious education, rather than the dogmatic or intellectual bias of Christian doctrine. Christian Living usually involved retreats, camps, group sessions on life situations, and community involvement. The practical and real aspects of Christian Living sought to appeal to students who were disillusioned with the aridity of the catechism. "Christian Living" lessons were not normally concerned with philosophical questions but rather the application of Christian teachings to ordinary life. One of the limits of this approach was the paucity of content. Many students felt that they had discussed to death how they felt about friendship, drugs, sex, and the latest films, but knew nothing about the magnificent heritage of the Christian story.

Christian Religious Education

Christian religious education is religious education that is explicitly Christian in its focus. Christian religious education situates its religious education firmly within the Jesus story and the values of the Christian community. Within the concept of Christian religious education, various churches have their own specific traditions. For example, Catholic religious education would have some specific dimensions, such as the doctrine of the communion of saints and the Real Presence, which have a particular meaning within this tradition. However, in the contemporary ecumenical climate, many themes in Christian religious education are common to the educational endeavors of all mainline Christian churches.

Goals of Religious Education

I propose the following goals for Christian religious education:

To develop a sense of personal worth within each person. All are created in the image of God.

To empower people to live with values that are derived from the ethical stance of Jesus Christ.

To assist in the celebration of liturgy, especially the eucharist.

To initiate members of the Christian community into the stories and wisdom of the Christian faith.

To raise consciousness of and provide opportunities for the realization of the kingdom of God through a just society.

To nurture the gift of imagination for the kingdom of God.

To become attuned to the beauty and mystery of creation.

To respond more actively to service of the poor.

To be open to search for truth through an exploration of God's revelation in the world.

To participate in the sacramental and prayerful life of the church.

To be more attuned to listening to God's word spoken through the bible, the teaching church, and the cultural environment.

To be recalled to a sense of sacred story in one's life journey and the life journey of others.

To grow in reconciliation through the transformation of failure.

To rejoice in the gospel of Jesus and share this gospel though evangelization and witness.

These goals of Christian education are stated in rather idealistic and general terms. However, each clarifies a particular dimension.

Conclusion

Over many centuries, the teaching of religion was a rather methodical process. The content of doctrine was clear and church teaching was formulated in the precise language of the catechism. However, rapid social changes, Vatican II church reforms, affluence for a few, growing poverty for many, and secularism are some of the influences that have challenged religious educators to evolve new styles of religious education, ones that are both faithful to student freedoms and the mission of the church to teach.

Religious truth is elusive. It cannot easily be expressed in clearly defined formulas because of the symbolic nature of religious language. Through our religious language forms, we are groping for ways to communicate the mystery of God's revelation in Jesus. If doctrines are separated from the religious experiences that generate them, they lose their power to mediate meaning for the religious tradition. The formulations themselves become sterile and irrelevant.

Ways to Respond

•Using your current text or other curriculum materials, make a list of all the essential religious truths included. Does your text also teach about other religions? Does it include Christian doctrine or lectionary catechesis?

•Try to become as familiar and as comfortable with the subject matter in your text as possible. Then choose the "name" (among the ones described in this chapter) that you think best describes what you teach.

•Make a list of your "goals" as a religious educator. Pray often for the grace to achieve them.

Questions for Reflection and/or Discussion

•Which of the approaches mentioned in this chapter do you now use in your teaching? If you teach in a parochial school, how would you describe your approach?

•Do those you teach need evangelization? Why or why not? Is catechesis your primary concern?

•Which aspects of catechesis do you consider most important?

•If you could impart to those you teach what you consider *essential* religious information, what would this include?

•What is your reaction to the author's goals of Christian religious education? Would you add any of your own?

Notes

Teaching Styles in Religious Education

Religion teachers may feel quite confident about their knowledge of the theology of a lesson but they regularly face two questions: How do I communicate this content? What teaching approaches are appropriate for this group? The students may be first communion children or sophomores in high school. The challenge is the same: How do I teach this topic effectively?

When I was first learning to teach religion, our student group at college was given a basic plan with four stages:

1) Introduce the topic by linking it with students' experiences, 2) Communicate the content (explanation, reading of text), 3) Initiate a process for learning the content (discussion, taking notes, drawing), and 4) Draw out implications for Christian living. Although many years have passed since I learned this, I can still recall the security it gave me in having at least one basic approach for planning and teaching my religion lessons.

Teaching is as old as humankind. Each generation has the responsibility of passing on to the next the wisdom of their age and the motivation to discover new horizons of knowledge. In recent years, teaching styles have been enriched by insights from the social sciences, especially psychology, sociology, and anthropology.

Teaching is an art, and teachers need to utilize every possible resource for maximum impact.

Eight Styles of Teaching

In this chapter I will describe eight styles of teaching religion. A style suggests a way of engaging in the process. The phases in each style or model are not steps in a lesson but rather movements of the flow of each lesson. Any experienced teacher knows that there are many variables in every learning situation. These include the time of the day, attitudes of the students, religious affiliations, climate of the school or parish, religious readiness of the group, and the teacher's knowledge and faith stance. I used to dread teaching religion on Friday afternoons or on windy days. The students just couldn't focus well on those occasions.

How teachers communicate the Christian story is perhaps as important as the story itself. Many a fumbling teacher has nevertheless left a lasting impression on students because of his or her deep faith. However, we should not excuse poor preparation or inept teaching because a teacher has faith. Both faith and an effective teaching style are necessary for good religious education.

Eight styles that incorporate learning theories

and principles of learning are: 1) Basic Movement, 2) Shared Praxis, 3) Contract, 4) Problem Solving, 5) Inquiry, 6) Concept Attainment, 7) Pastoral Experience, and 8) Peer Learning.

Let us consider each of these styles or models and illustrate each by using a theme.

Model 1: Basic Movement
(*Theme:* Caring for Earth)

Encounter: The topic is introduced by linking it to the life experiences of the students, for example, for the topic, "Care for Earth," students are presented with such questions as: What are your experiences of care or lack of care for Earth? What do you do to help (not help) the environment? Then listen to a song about Earth.

Exploration: Study the theme "Caring for Earth." Use research, exposition, film, discussion of a Christian theology of earth.

Depthing: Examples of the process of going deeper into a topic would be: making a collage, discussion, having a panel of speakers, giving a report.

Christian Focus: Exploration of responses to the theme from a Christian perspective: How is care for Earth related to my life as a Christian? What is my Christian response now?

Model 2: Shared Praxis
(*Theme:* Prejudice and the Book of Jonah)

Life Experience: Ask students: When have you met a situation of prejudice? What happened? Discuss this.

Reflection: Allow students to recall and savor their experiences of prejudice and get in touch with their feelings.

Christian Story: Explain the book of Jonah as a story about prejudice. The background to the book is post-exilic Israel, which is trying to rebuild its identity by setting rigid boundaries of inclusion and exclusion.

Appropriation: Through a process of reflecting on the stories of the students and the Christian story, the group is led to identify ele-

ments of prejudice and to interiorize the significance of the Jonah story for today.

Sharing: Each member of the group is encouraged to break down some of the prejudices that she or he experiences.

Model 3: Contract
(*Theme:* A gospel study)

Focus: A group of people meet with an expectation of learning more about the gospels. The leader helps the group clarify their intentions and come to decisions about the time and place of the meetings, the exact theme, for example, "The Gospel of Mark," and resources that are available to the group.

Participation: The group meets to study the Gospel of Mark. The learning process is faithful to the contract which has been agreed upon in the "focus" stage.

Evaluation: After the contracted sessions have been completed, the group evaluates the effectiveness of the contract.

Modification: In light of the evaluation, a new contract is developed for further gospel studies, or the group may choose to disband.

Model 4: Problem Solving
(*Theme:* Christian forgiveness)

Problem Posed: A problem is selected or arises out of a discussion with the group, for example: Is Christian forgiveness possible?

Analysis: Exploration of various dimensions of the problem: Do people really forgive? Does history teach us anything about forgiveness?

Research: Trace the theme in scripture, religious traditions, film, literature, or history.

Formulation: Formulate a statement from the group based on a critique of research on Christian forgiveness. Is Christian forgiveness really possible?

Model 5: Inquiry
(*Theme:* Rituals)

Focus: The theme of the inquiry is mutually agreed upon.

Experience: The group reflects on rituals that

they have experienced: Graduation day, Earth day, Thanksgiving, Orientation day.

Research: The group investigates various sacred rituals: the passover meal, funeral services, a bar mitzvah, the eucharistic liturgy. The elements of these rituals are identified.

Verification: The findings of the research are tested against research on other sacred rituals.

Location: The group then composes a religious ritual for an end-of-the-school-year ceremony.

Model 6: Concept Attainment
(*Theme:* Covenant)

Identification of the concept "covenant."

Gathering Perceptions: Students are invited to share their understandings of and stories about relationships and promises.

Investigation: Using a variety of resources, such as texts, dictionaries, and readings, the group examines various meanings of "covenant." Characteristics of the concept of covenant are listed from this research.

Articulation: Using the data gained from the research, students make a first attempt to define the concept of covenant. Students then test their definition of covenant against their research findings.

Insight: Students examine the process of how they reached a definition of a religious concept. They then discuss how this process might help them to approach other religious questions.

Model 7: Field Experience
(*Theme:* Christian service)

Orientation: The group discusses a forthcoming field experience, clarifying the purpose and details of the excursion.

Field Study: Visitation for a field study. Places for field study may be such centers as senior housing, a home for disabled people, a shelter for the homeless, or a soup kitchen.

Report and Debriefing: Sharing of observations and issues arising from the field study.

Christian Reflection: If appropriate, the group might be invited to discuss the implications of their observations for their Christian lives.

Model 8: Peer Learning
(*Theme:* Friendship)

Focus on the theme.

Group Search: Small peer groups are constituted to research the theme.

Forum: Each peer group shares insights with other groups in a general forum.

Extension: Peer learning groups are re-formed to extend the scope of their inquiry to consider a Christian approach to friendship.

Synthesis: Small peer groups combine again to formulate key ideas on the theme by incorporating the various ideas from the groups and the forum.

These eight models or styles are not lesson plans but rather directions for the learning process. They should be employed with flexibility and sensitivity to specific groups according to levels of readiness.

Learning Strategies

A further aspect of teaching religion is the utilization of a wide variety of strategies for the learning process. These include telling stories, making collages and mobiles, mood painting, song and dance, music, mime, drama, research, interviews, panels, field studies, composing video and audio tapes, roleplay, peer learning, journal keeping, composition of rituals, nature walks, creative writing, and active imagination exercises.

Experienced teachers will choose strategies that are appropriate for their group and take into account such factors as the mood of the group, availability of resources, age, physical environment, and the time of day or night. Teachers need to be aware of the various personality types who are participating: introverts, extroverts, sensing, intuitive, thinking, or feeling types (as explained by the Myers-Briggs personality indicators). No one activity is going to suit everyone, so a teacher should try to have a range of activities that will appeal to sensing, feeling, thinking, and intuiting types in the class.

Also some of these strategies may not sit comfortably with teachers. Although a teacher should try to employ the best possible strategies, one should not forget that Christian religious education can never simply be a social science activity. Rather, it is a movement of the Spirit. Hence, religion teachers have to be persons who regularly pray for and with their students.

Planning Techniques

For those whose responsibility it is to co-ordinate religious education programs in parishes or schools, there should be an awareness of a number of elements that constitute a sound program with an explicit Christian ethos. I propose the following areas of concern as meriting attention by DREs and principals:

Communications: All the teaching staff, parents, and students should be informed about the program and its philosophy.

Climate: The program should reflect the Christian spirit of the parish or school. Gospel values ought to be evident in the whole atmosphere. Religious education is an expression of the ethos of the parish or school.

Participation: All staff should be involved at some appropriate level in the program though participation in such activities as retreats, assemblies, liturgical preparation, social justice projects, and for some staff, the explicit teaching activity itself.

Personal Development: All staff should be given opportunities to grow in spirituality and insight into the faith journey.

Curriculum: A comprehensive religious education curriculum should be planned through liaison with the diocesan guidelines and the needs of the local student population.

Resources: Appropriate resources should be accessible to catechists, teachers, DREs, and principals.

Evaluation: There should be regular evaluations of the program, with ongoing modifications according to the nature of the feedback.

Parents: Parents should be invited to participate through such activities as providing resource people, input into the curriculum, engagement in adult faith development, serving on religious education committees, assisting on retreats and field trips, leading in prayer services, and contacting people within the wider group of parents.

Leadership: The parish and school leaders should be enthusiastic and active in promoting their programs and should work hard at keeping communication open between parents, students, and staff.

Christ Focus: The person of Jesus should be the inspiration and foundation stone of the whole religious education enterprise.

Staff Relations: Relationships among staff should be caring and cooperative. The quality of staff relations witnesses to the integrity of gospel values within the parish or school community.

Action for Justice: The program should include activities that enhance human dignity and work for a more just world.

Celebration: The parish or school community should celebrate the good news through worship services, liturgy, and prayer services.

Flexibility: The program should be an authentic response to the needs of the students and should be modified accordingly on an ongoing basis.

Ecclesial: The program should be an extension and expression of the church's mission to teach. Students and teachers should be encouraged to live out gospel values by their care and compassion toward each other.

These dimensions of religion programs offer a wholistic view as to how religious education should be approached and evaluated. Administrators need to have a comprehensive perspective on the whole enterprise lest the immediacy of the task lead to a loss of vision.

Conclusion

Teaching religion should open new doors and support students in shaping a future of hope. It seeks to engage students in revisioning religious symbols and extending their reality by acknowledging God's place in it.

A religion teacher is an artist, fashioning a new creation, spurred on by the belief that something unique is there in the depths, waiting for the artist's imagination to call it into being. By offering these styles and models of teaching, I am not implying that there is any comfortable recipe for the communication of religious truth. Catechists and teachers walk across sacred ground when they venture into the mystery of revealing God to their students. They must walk this ground lightly for two reasons: 1) God is the one who speaks to hearts, not the religion teacher, and 2) the hopes and dreams of students can be so fragile.

Ways to Respond

•Using the eight models of teaching described in this chapter, plan eight sessions on the theme "peace." Note how you would develop this theme in each of these models: 1. Basic Style, 2. Shared Praxis, 3. Contract, 4. Problem Solving, 5. Inquiry, 6. Concept Attainment, 7. Pastoral Experience, and 8. Peer Learning.

•Keep a diary of your lesson approaches. Which approach has been most effective? Why?

•Imagine that you are the one responsible for the administration of your parish or school religion program. Make a list of 10 principles that would guide your planning.

•Plan a lesson on the theme of "reconciliation." Evaluate the lesson with another teacher.

Questions for Reflection and/or Discussion

•What has been the most creative teaching experience you have ever had? How did your students respond? Why was it memorable for you?

•Do you ever question the directions in your textbook? Do they always fit your personal teaching style? Are they appropriate for your particular group? Why or why not?

•Which of the eight styles of teaching discussed in this chapter do you relate to best? Are there any you have not tried? Are you willing to branch out?

•Do you use a variety of learning strategies in every lesson? Which are your favorites?

•Do you feel that the areas of concern described in this chapter fit your religion program? Why or why not?

Notes

Chapter 6

Teaching about the Bible

The bible is the most influential book in history. The word "bible" means "the books." It has two sections, the Old Testament and the New Testament. The word testament is derived from a Hebrew word meaning covenant. Out of respect for the Jewish people, we tend today to use the word "Hebrew Scriptures" for the Old Testament. Thus the New Testament is often referred to as the Christian Scriptures.

The bible is a composition of 46 books in the Old Testament or Hebrew Scriptures and 27 books in the New Testament. The Jewish people and Protestants recognize 40 books that were written in Hebrew. Catholics recognize a further six books written in Greek. The church gradually came to recognize a certain number of books as constituting the canon of the scriptures. By the year 367 C.E., the number of books in the New Testament was confirmed as 27.

The Council of Trent (1545-1563) specified the "canon" (officially accepted books) of the Old Testament. The books of the Old Testament are a mix of epics, poetry, prayers, prophecy, history, proverbs, primal myths, court chronicles, and wise sayings. The period covered by much of the Old Testament extends from the call of Abraham (c. 1800 B.C.E.) to the first century before Christ. The Old Testament was originally written in Hebrew and translated into Greek in the beginning of the third century B.C.E.

The New Testament was written in Greek. In 1226 the bible was divided into chapters, and in 1551 the chapters were further divided into verses for the convenience of locating biblical passages.

The New Testament is a theological reflection on the person and mission of Christ and the early Christian community. The four gospels of Matthew, Mark, Luke, and John offer four portraits of Jesus from the perspectives of four early Christian communities. The New Testament contains 21 letters written to Christian communities. Paul is named as the author of 13 of these letters although it is doubtful if he wrote more than nine of them. Luke's second book, the Acts of the Apostles, is an absorbing account of life in early Christian communities during the period of thirty years after the death of Jesus. The New Testament concludes with the book of Revelation, a book of hope about the eventual triumph of God over the evil forces of persecution.

In this century, there have been enormous gains in our knowledge of the bible. Archeology, literary criticism, history, and linguistics have enabled us to better appreciate the texts by illuminating the social and religious context of the biblical writings. The marriage of scientific studies with theology has been a fruitful one. Until recently, the church's suspicion and rejection of scientific research into biblical times impoverished our knowledge of biblical texts and reduced Christians to biblical fundamentalists.

The bible is a book of faith in which we learn about God's revelation to us. Christians believe that it is inspired. Biblical inspiration understands God as the source of inspiration, and in this sense we speak of God as the "primary author." The human writers of the biblical text are referred to as "instrumental authors" and write from their historical frame of reference. Hence a reader of the texts must take into account such factors as the time of writing, the place of writing, the purpose of the book, and the theology of the author and community.

Teaching the bible offers many opportunities for a creative teacher to allow the Word of God to become alive in the hearts of students. The following approaches may help stimulate interest in the bible as a book for life.

Listening to God's Word

Isaiah (55:10-11) describes the cycle of the Word of God moving mysteriously through all creation and returning to its source. Jesus draws upon this imagery in his parable of the sower and the seed where the scattered seed evokes six possible reactions, ranging from the waste of the seed which is taken by the birds, to the hundred-fold fertility. God's spoken word may be rendered sterile by rejection or inattention, or it may bring forth abundant fruit by an enthusiastic response to God's invitation to grow into love (Mark 4:1-9). When Jesus had finished telling the parable he cried out: "Anyone who has ears for listening should listen!"

If teaching of the bible is to influence the quality of Christian living, then the atmosphere of the classroom should be conducive to listening and contemplation. The room should be

so arranged that the bible is placed in a central position with candles, flowers, and other symbols of the Word of God. Reverent silence, breathing exercises, playing of soft music, comfortable positions for prayer, all may be conducive to experiencing the Word of God in the heart as well as in the head. The saying of mantras such as: "Jesus, come to me," "Lord that I may see," "Father, Son, and Spirit," may allow our biblical prayer to resonate with our breathing. To help students appreciate the bible, the teacher could introduce this simple meditation style:

• Become quiet.
• Pray to the Spirit.
• Read a short passage from scripture.
• Allow a word or phrase to stay in your consciousness.
• Explore the significance of this word or phrase.
• Pose the question: Why is this thought important to my Christian life now?
• Pray for guidance.
• Offer thanksgiving.

The scripture passage used might be the gospel reading for the liturgy of the following Sunday. For young children certain words should be simplified.

Getting into the Text

How are students helped to meet Jesus in the gospels? I would like to propose a process to help this encounter, using the story of Zacchaeus (Luke 19:1-10).

First read the text carefully. Jesus entered Jericho and was going through the town and suddenly a man whose name was Zacchaeus made his appearance; he was one of the senior tax collectors and a wealthy man. He kept trying to see Jesus, but he was too short and could not see him over the crowd, so he ran ahead and climbed a sycamore tree to catch a glimpse of Jesus who was to pass that way. When Jesus reached the spot he looked up and spoke to him, "Zacchaeus, come down. Hurry, because I am to stay at your house today." And he hurried down and welcomed Jesus joyfully. The people complained when they saw what was happening. "He has gone to stay at a sinner's house," they said. But Zacchaeus stood his ground and said to the Lord, "Look, sir, I am going to give half my property to the poor, and if I have cheated people I will pay them back four times the amount." And Jesus said to him, "Today salvation has come to this house, because this man, too, is a son of Abraham; for the Son of man has come to seek out and save what was lost."

Reflect on the text. Let the words and phrases convey their own power to the students. Examine the relationships between words and the structure of the story. Invite students to underline words that impress them or highlight name words or phrases like "hurry," "glimpse of Jesus." Invite them to share their feelings about the passage.

Look at the social, religious, and political background of the story. Jesus spent much of his life around the northern part of the sea of Galilee. The political climate might be described as a tinderbox of frustrated nationalist sentiments ready to explode against the occupying Roman armies. The zealots were the revolutionary group. The Roman military presence was strengthened after the revolt of Judas the Galilean and his followers. The uprising was put down with special ferocity by the Roman commander, Varus. Jesus was about ten years old at the time of this insurrection, and the sight of crucified Jews on the hills of Galilee must have made a deep impression on him. Almost certainly, relatives of Jesus would have been involved in the revolt.

The high priests had been corrupted by their collaboration with the Romans and were regarded as traitors by the nationalists. The synagogues had become the religious centers of Palestine, although the temple in Jerusalem, which had been rebuilt by Herod, was still a symbol of a bygone golden era in Judaism. The Sadducees saw themselves as the upholders of the written law and rejected any oral interpretations.

They were representative of the rich and powerful, and they jealously guarded their privileged position and moved quickly to eliminate any threat to their social and religious status.

The Pharisees were not fundamentalists, and apart from the Torah, they recognized the *Halakah* or exposition of the law. The Pharisees sought to uphold the spirit of the law, but faced with the threats of erosion of beliefs and persecution from without, they had difficulty developing a coherent religious relationship with the marginalized, especially after the destruction of Jerusalem in 70 C.E.

After the sacking of Jerusalem, the Sadducees, Zealots, and the Essene religious sect were swallowed up by the Roman juggernaut. The Pharisees alone remained to begin the task of rebuilding the Jewish religion. Some scripture scholars suggest that Jesus was closest to the Pharisees in spirit but differed with them on a number of issues, such as interpreting the law of the Sabbath and inclusion of outsiders.

The Pharisees get very bad press in the gospels, especially from John and Matthew. Both gospels were written at the time of the acrimonious breach between the followers of Jesus and the mother religion of Judaism. After the Pharisee council of Jamnia in 85 C.E., the break was complete. The fledgling Christian community was on its own. The bitterness of the division between the Pharisees and the early Christian community led John and Matthew especially to cast the Pharisees as villains in the death of Jesus. Christian anti-semitism was spawned and has ever since been a lurking monster in the shadow side of the Christian story.

The Meaning of Kingdom

At the time of Jesus, the term "kingdom of God" had at least four meanings. One understanding was a political view that the kingdom of Israel would be restored by throwing off oppressors by armed revolt. This movement would be a kind of return to the glory of David's kingdom. The Zealots taught this version of the kingdom of God. The Essenes awaited the inauguration of a transcendent universal kingdom for the chosen ones of Light. The Pharisees believed that the kingdom would be established by strict adherence to the Torah and righteous living. Jesus proclaimed a kingdom for all those who were willing to establish a relationship with God as *Abba*, beloved father, and become a community of compassion.

In the story of Zacchaeus, Jesus would have stunned and even scandalized the Jericho community. Zacchaeus, as a senior tax collector, was a ritual outcast. To choose an outcast as the host for table fellowship would have outraged the righteous. To add insult to injury, Jesus named Zacchaeus a "son of Abraham." Such an affirmation challenged the carefully structured religious categories of people according to the Torah. The action of Jesus was a threat that the religious authorities could not ignore. And they did not. He was apprehended and murdered not many months after his encounter with Zacchaeus.

Because it is so important, let's trace the four movements of this story. They speak to us about the theology of the passage.

1) The first movement indicates the separation of Zacchaeus from Jesus by the hostile and prejudiced crowd. 2) In the second movement, Jesus and Zacchaeus meet and are surrounded by a hostile crowd. 3) In the third movement, Jesus and Zacchaeus go off together to share a meal. 4) In the fourth movement, table fellowship is experienced and the community celebrates an outsider coming home.

These movements of the story speak to us about four stages in our own encounter with Jesus. We may have obstacles in trying to meet him, but we must take risks (go out on a limb for Jesus!) if we wish to break through the barriers to experience his hospitality.

Consider the following ways to share this story with your students.

Express the biblical story in "colors" that reflect its various moods. For example, the mood of Zacchaeus in the morning before he met Jesus might be painted as purple with some streaks of yellow to suggest excitement. Meeting Jesus could be painted as a blaze of oranges and reds, with green as an envy color to catch the mood of the crowd. Table fellowship might be painted as pink, white, and blue. Mood coloring helps students enter scripture stories emotionally.

Re-tell the story with vitality and imagination. You might begin like this...

Zacchaeus, a senior tax collector in Jericho, was puzzled. He paced up and down the terrace of his beautiful home wondering what he should do. The merchants of Jericho had told him that the miracle worker, Jesus of Nazareth, was due in Jericho that day. Zacchaeus dearly wanted to see this Jesus, but he dreaded another rejection. The townsfolk were divided about Jesus. Some said he was a dangerous rabble-rouser who would only bring the Roman iron fist upon the town. Others said he was very kind, especially to outsiders like Zacchaeus. His wife warned him not to risk the wrath of the crowd by going into town. What was he to do?

Depict the story in the form of collages, drawings, mobiles, sculpture, stained-glass windows, or portraits. Drawings sketched with the minimum of detail are effective. Encourage students to find as many ways as possible to personally and creatively depict the story.

Invite students to become the various characters of the story and reflect how each feels. For example, ask in reference to Zacchaeus: When have you been a Zacchaeus character? When have you felt like an outsider and not been invited into a group? When have you been alienated or rejected? How have you felt when someone welcomed you in?

In reference to the crowd ask: When have I judged people? When have I excluded others because of their reputation? When have I stereotyped others because of their ethnic identity, education, or profession?

In reference to Jesus ask: When have I acted as Jesus did and reached out to accept people as they are? When have I praised others and made them feel worthwhile?

Present the scripture story in contemporary terms. For example, a modern version of this story might be about a new high school student who is excluded from the peer group because the other students discover that his or her father is in prison. However, one of the class refuses to accept the peer group's exclusion and befriends the new student.

Imaginatively reflect on a scripture story from the perspective of what happened before and after. For example, in the story of the cure of the ten lepers (Luke 17:11-19), in the scene before the ten lepers might have been discussing their hopes about meeting Jesus. After the cure, nine of the lepers would disappear from the scene without saying thanks, while the one Samaritan went back to thank Jesus. Each of the lepers might express why they did or did not offer thanks to Jesus after being cured from this terrible scourge.

In the Zacchaeus story, student imaginations might carry them to the house of the Zacchaeus family where they are discussing Jesus before he arrives. After the encounter with Jesus, their imaginations can help them explore the nervousness of some of the disciples about being in the house of a ritually unclean person. Also they can listen while Zacchaeus gently breaks the news to his wife about their dramatically reduced family finances!

Here are some additional creative responses:
- Invite the class to draw a symbol of the story or compose a motto for it.
- Nominate five characters "from the crowd" to retell the story, each from his or her own point of view.
- Compose a biblical song or hymn based on the story.
- Mime or roleplay the story.
- Make a video or cassette tape by interviewing the various characters in the story.
- Discuss a theme related to the story like prej-
udice, racism, or stereotypes in society.
- Compose and celebrate a prayer service based on the story. Include songs, movement, readings, prayers, and symbols.
- Write poetry, short stories, or diaries based on the story.

Meeting Jesus

For Christians, the God-event of the incarnation is the most important happening in world history. "The Word was made flesh and he lived among us" (John 1:14). The books of the New Testament are reflections from early Christian communities about Jesus and his Way. The ideas offered here may help students to encounter the Jesus of the New Testament.

Jesus asked this question of his disciples. "Who do you say I am?" (Mark 8:29). If we wish to understand the person of Jesus, we need to ask this question of ourselves. Through listening to our innermost thoughts and feelings, we discover the depths of our humanity. We also grow into the wholeness of our being by sensitive interpersonal relationships. We recognize our need to give and receive love, to experience intimacy, to be challenged and affirmed. During our lives, we strive to modify our dreams and reconcile the paradoxes.

Once we develop a sense of the journey and the story of our own life, we are better able to move on to the life story of Jesus and return with an enriched insight into our own story. I suggest that there are four stages in the process of moving on and returning with insight. I model these on three movements developed by John Dunne, as described in his book *A Search for God in Time and Memory* (see Suggested Resources). I have added the fourth. The activity of moving on to the life of Jesus is a journey of insight into the stages and passages of our own lives. The four phases of the process are as follows:

1. Reflecting on our own lives, especially key passage times.

2. Passing over or moving on to key passage times in the life of Jesus.

3. Returning with insight into our own lives.

4. Moving into another depth of communion with God, ourselves, others, and Earth, based on this experience.

Jesus came to be with us as Emmanuel so as to share our broken human condition and transform it by his saving presence. Jesus is the archetypal person for every woman and man. By passing across from our own life situation to the events and experiences of the life of Jesus, we can be affirmed and challenged to enhance the quality of our own lives.

The Archetypal Hero

Another way to view the life of Jesus is from the perspective of the "archetypal hero." In myths, legends, and folk tales, the hero or heroine lives a life characterized by such features as birth in humble circumstances, receiving a core insight, leaving the family and going on a journey, sharing insight, gathering a community to proclaim these insights, meeting opposition, often in a violent form, receiving help, sometimes unexpectedly, suffering rejection and ultimately death, living on in spirit within the community.

The life of Jesus corresponds with the features of the life of the archetypal hero or heroine. Such an approach may assist students in appreciating Jesus as the cosmic Christ who is a hero for all people in all cultures. The lives of many famous people, as well as heroines and heroes of mythology, illustrate the characteristics of the archetypal person. Consider for example, Odysseus, Gilgamesh, or Robin Hood.

In telling the story of Jesus as archetypal hero, a teacher may use the following texts:

Luke 2:1-14, born in the humble environment of a stable

Mark 3:31-35, left his family

Mark 4:1-11, received a core insight

Mark 1:16-20, gathered a community

Mark 3:22-30, encountered opposition

Luke 10:1-16, empowered his followers

Mark 15:33-39, met a violent death

Luke 24:1-8, was raised from the dead

Luke 24:44-53, returned to the Father after sending the disciples on mission

A third way to view Jesus is as the keeper of dreams. A dream is a basic hope or vision that gives people a life orientation and is a source of core values. Our dreams influence our priorities and shape our horizons. Dreams grow and are modified according to our environment. Like any vital adult, Jesus pursued his dream with passion. The kingdom of God or reign of God is mentioned by Jesus 91 times in the gospels. Mark's Gospel records that Jesus began his ministry by announcing the good news of the reign of God (Mark 1:14-15).

A study of the gospels reveals the following features of the dream of Jesus:

Luke 11:1-13, a new relationship with God as *Abba*

Luke 19:1-10, table fellowship that was inclusive of everyone

Matthew 25:31-46, compassionate justice for the outsiders

Matthew 13:24-30, living with the ambivalence of good and evil

Matthew 13:44-45, the priority of the quest for the kingdom

Mark 4:26-29, the mystery of how the kingdom grows

Luke 17:21, the immediacy of the kingdom

Matthew 5:23, reconciliation as a sign of the spirit of the kingdom

Help students reflect on their own dreams and the dreams of famous people in history. Explorers, saints, crusaders for human rights, artists, and scientists have followed their dreams to create a better world. A conversion to the dream of Jesus involves a radical shift in our horizons. Being a kingdom person suggests one who is open to the imaginative possibilities of living differently.

Have students study the images of Jesus, who described himself using these images:

"I am the vine, you are the branches" (John 15:5).

"I am the living bread which has come down from heaven" (John 6:51).

"I am the light of the world" (John 8:12).

"I am the good shepherd" (John 10:14).

"I am the resurrection" (John 11:26).

"I am the gate of the sheepfold" (John 10:7).

In the Hebrew Scriptures, God is presented in such images as fire, cloud, rock, eagle, shepherd, potter, and mother.

Encourage students to explore biblical images by reflecting on some of the dimensions of the image, for example the shepherd image of Jesus might be developed as one who knows the sheep in an intimate way; who guards the sheep against dangers; who is faithful; who leads the sheep to pasture; who carries the lost sheep home on his shoulder; who allows the sheep to graze in green pastures.

Invite students to compose their own images of God or Jesus and have them explain the significance of these images. Encourage them, too, to imagine a modern-day Jesus. What if Jesus were here today? What kind of person would Jesus be if he lived here in our own country? Contemporary people who exhibit "Jesus" qualities in their lives can help students imagine the possible lifestyle Jesus might have today. Where would he live? What would he say and do? Students will certainly provide teachers with a few surprises and much insight with their perceptions about Jesus.

Study Bible Themes

Another way of teaching the bible is to select a theme and research the references and significance of the theme in the scriptures. Some key biblical themes are water, mountains, journey, covenant, land, and redemption. To illustrate how these themes may be used in teaching the bible, I have selected three of them for brief comment.

1. Water: The Jewish people were influenced by two separate traditions of water. The sojourn in Egypt had taught them about water as life. The mighty Nile river was the religious and economic heart of the great kingdom of the pharaohs. Its regular waters replenished the fertile spaces of the Egyptian heartland. To the East, the meandering Tigris and Euphrates rivers frequently flooded the flat plains of Babylon.

Within Palestine itself, the sea of Galilee was the source of fish, but its violent storms caused many deaths among fishermen. Water was both life and chaos in Jewish mythology. John's Gospel draws upon the symbol of water as life to express the saving ministry of Jesus (John 19:34). Water flows from the side of Jesus when a soldier pierces it with a spear.

Water as life is the backdrop for the connection between Jesus and the woman at Jacob's well. Jesus cries out about his power to be living water: "Let anyone who is thirsty come to me!" (John 7:37). Crossing a body of water symbolized entering a new life. The crossing of the Sea of Reeds during the Exodus marked the beginning of a new phase in the story of God's chosen people. In baptism, water symbolizes the beginning of a new life through initiation into the Christian community.

2. Mountains: This is a universal religious symbol. On mountains, people encounter God. They evoke feelings of awe, mystery, timelessness, and wilderness. In the bible, mountains are very important places. One might almost say that the main biblical themes are associated with mountain experiences. Consider the following encounters.

Old Testament: Noah's ark on the mountain of Ararat (Genesis 8:4), Abraham's sacrifice (Genesis 22), Moses and the burning bush on the mountain of Horeb (Exodus 3:1-6), Moses and the covenant on mount Sinai (Exodus 19:16-25).

New Testament: Jesus and the mount of temptations (Matthew 4:8), Jesus teaching on the mount of Beatitudes (Matthew 5:1-12), the transfiguration (Luke 9:28-36), the death of Jesus on Calvary (Luke 23:33), the mount of the Ascension (Matthew 28:16).

Students might be asked to discuss their own experiences of mountains and their feelings about being on a mountain. Research into various religions illuminates the importance of mountains in religious mythology.

3. Journeys: The biblical journey describes the journey for every person with its seasons, crises, and passages. In the biblical journey, we discover God, and we learn that there is grace in making the journey as well as in arriving.

Consider these biblical journeys: Abraham to Bethel, Moses and the Hebrews to the promised land, Joshua crossing the Jordan river, David to the city of Jerusalem, Elijah to Mount Horeb, Tobias to Media, the people of Jerusalem to and from the exile, Joseph and Mary to Egypt, the journey of the Magi, the last great journey of Jesus toward Jerusalem, the Emmaus journey, Paul to Asia Minor and to Rome.

The Exodus and the Emmaus journeys, described below, are two special ones that describe many significant dimensions of the faith journey.

1. The Exodus journey is a story of fidelity, despair, hope, and betrayal. Moses leads his people from a place of slavery to freedom. Slowly and painfully, the nomads are forged into a community who are bonded by a covenant. Leaving Egypt was a risk. When the desert winds buffeted the straggling travelers, Egypt, bad as it was, became very desirable. But there was no turning back from the commitment to follow the cloud of Yahweh. Manna on the way (Exodus 16:18) provided food for the journey, and the surprise of water from the rock reminded the disheartened people that God's providence was always near (Exodus 17:6).

The Exodus journey affirms and challenges us to be faithful to a belief that God travels with us, even when events seem to turn against us. The refrain "Do not take fright, do not be afraid" might well be our own treasured saying as we continue along the way.

2. The Emmaus journey is described in Luke's Gospel, Chapter 24. Two disciples leave Jerusalem carrying the pain of broken dreams. Their hopes in Jesus have evaporated in light of his brutal death. Suddenly a stranger catches up to them and they pour out their hearts to him. When the stranger responds to their stories of despair, the two disciples slowly begin to comprehend the mystery of suffering within the sal-

vation story. During the experience of table fellowship later that day, bread is broken and suddenly the disciples realize: "It is the Lord!" They hurry back to Jerusalem with great joy to share the resurrection experience.

Little wonder that Emmaus is such a favorite story for Christians. How often have we pondered the place of failure and suffering? What does it mean? How can it be transformed into resurrection? When has the Lord walked with us as stranger?

Biblical themes help students draw together many loose threads and offer guidelines for relating scripture to real life experiences. The theme chosen needs to be appropriate for the religious readiness of the students.

Creativity and the Bible

Teaching the bible provides many opportunities for creative approaches such as creative writing and poetry, keeping journals based on the journal of Paul, writing plays or newspaper articles. Mime, dance, drama, statue drama, and free drama are other ways to approach scripture. Some biblical stories especially suited for dramatic presentation are the book of Jonah, the creation story, Noah, David and Nathan, Peter's denial of Jesus, and the parable of the prodigal son.

Other creative activities include music as song, musicals, hymns, the singing of psalms, and art forms like mobiles, symbols, stained-glass windows, color impressions, and collages.

Biblical Exegesis

Students may be helped to understand the bible by an examination of the literary genre of the writings, the historical context of the books, the various theories about the composition and authors of the books. In teaching the gospels, it would be imperative that students learn about the three stages in the evolution of the gospel texts.

The first stage was the ministry of Jesus (circa 30 C.E.). The next stage was the kerygma or preaching the good news (circa 65 C.E.). The third stage was the composition of the gospels of Mark, Luke, Matthew, and John (circa 100 C.E.). Each of the gospels reflects the theology of four early Christian communities. Archaeology and history are uncovering many long buried secrets of the biblical era. Biblical exegesis assists students to develop a methodology for reflecting on the scriptures.

Conclusion

The bible may be studied at many different levels. At the personal level, the bible is studied as a book that offers insight into life situations. At the intellectual level, it is examined from the perspectives of form criticism, redaction, and historical composition. At the social level, it is a guide to a critique of society and moral behavior. At the ecumenical level, the Christian bible is a book of scriptures that may be compared with the scriptures of other great religions such as the Koran of Islam or the Vedas of the Hindu tradition. The level of study is usually determined by the purpose of the bible lesson. Of course, a number of levels may be included in any given lesson.

Christians believe that God is revealed through the bible. Teaching it with imagination, creativity, and relevance will help students to meet the mysterious God of the biblical story who is portrayed as Emmanuel, God with us, and Companion to us along the way.

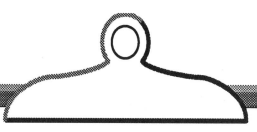

Ways to Respond

•Encourage your students to produce a one-page newspaper that describes a particular biblical event. Below are sample articles.

PILATE ISSUES WARNING

Governor Pontius Pilate today issued a communique from his fortress warning that any lawlessness or riots would be ruthlessly suppressed. During the last few weeks, Roman soldiers have been observed moving into stations around the city. "The Roman soldier is well prepared for any emergency," said Pilate.

NEW ATTACKS ON JERICHO ROAD

Jericho: At least three robberies took place yesterday on the Jerusalem-Jericho road. One victim was so badly wounded that he died a short time after the attack. It is believed that he could have been saved had any of the travelers stopped to render aid and stop the bleeding.

CAMELS CAMELS CAMELS

Sturdy strong beasts. Best prices in town. Selling for only 58 drachmas each. Apply: Jacob Hosea, No. 14 Camel Yard, Jerusalem.

•In your personal journal or notebook, write your own description of Jesus as if it were a profile for a newspaper. Include everything you would want your students to know about Jesus.

Questions for Reflection and/or Discussion

•How much do you know about the bible? Have you ever taken a scripture course? If not, is it possible to organize one in your parish, for catechists, teachers, and interested parents? (Talk to your DRE, pastor, or principal.)

•What is your favorite way to present the bible to those you teach? How do your students respond?

•Do you ever offer students quiet reflection time to ponder scripture passages?

•What are your favorite scripture verses? How do you make use of them in your teaching?

Notes

Teaching about Prayer

The disciples begged Jesus: "Lord, teach us to pray" (Luke 11:1). Many students look to their catechists and teachers for this same kind of guidance. But first of all, what is prayer? It is an expression of our relationship with God. In prayer we allow God to meet us at the core of our being. The bible has many images of prayer and it is important to reflect on these before trying to teach about prayer. Consider the following in particular, and spend time reflecting on them as you prepare to teach others about prayer.

The Lord seeks to enter our lives: "Look, I am standing at the door, knocking. If one of you hears me calling and opens the door, I will come in to share a meal with you" (Revelation 3:20-21).

People experience longing for God: "As a deer yearns for running streams, so I yearn for you my God. I thirst for God, the living God; when shall I go to see the face of God?" (Psalm 42:1-3).

We beg God to hear our pleas: "Ask, and it will be given to you, search and you will find, knock, and the door will be opened to you" (Luke 11:9-10).

We need to make space for God's presence: "But when you pray, go to your private room and shut the door, and so pray to your Father who is in that secret place" (Matthew 6:6).

"In the morning, long before dawn, he got up and left the house, and went off to a lonely place and prayed there" (Mark 1:35).

We must allow the indwelling of God to happen: "Those who love me will keep my word, and my Father will love them, and we shall come to them and make a home with them" (John 14:23).

Wrestling with God is part of life: "And going on a little further, he threw himself on the ground and prayed that, if if were possible, this hour might pass him by. 'Abba' (Father) he said, 'for you everything is possible. Take this cup away from me. But let it be as you, not I, would have it'" (Mark 14:35-36).

We need to trust in God: "I hold myself in quiet and silence like a child in its mother's arms, like a child, so I keep myself" (Psalm 131:2).

We all need to ask for forgiveness: "Have mercy on me, O God, in your faithful love, in your great tenderness wipe away my offenses; wash me thoroughly from my guilt, purify me from my sin" (Psalm 51:1-2).

We must come to terms with God's will: "Mary said, 'You see before you the Lord's servant, let it happen to me as you have said'" (Luke 1:38).

Jesus cried out in a loud voice saying "Father, into your hands I commit my Spirit" (Luke 23:46).

We should give thanks: "Father I thank you for hearing my prayer. I myself know that you always hear me" (John 11:42).

We should praise God: "I will bless Yahweh at all times, his praise will be continually on my lips. I will praise Yahweh from my heart; let the humble hear and rejoice" (Psalm 34:1-2).

We should joyfully celebrate creation: "Glory to Yahweh forever; may Yahweh find joy in all creatures! At Yahweh's glance the earth trembles, and at God's touch the mountains pour forth smoke! I shall sing to Yahweh all my life, make music for my God as long as I live" (Psalm 104:31-33).

Union with God is our goal: "I am the vine, you are the branches. Whoever remains in me, with me in him bears fruit in plenty" (John 15:5).

We long for God's love: "May God through the spirit enable you to grow firm in power with regard to your inner self, so that Christ may live in your hearts through faith. Then planted in love and built on love, with all God's holy people you will have the strength to grasp the breadth and the length, the height and the depth; so that knowing the love of Christ, which is beyond all knowledge, you may be filled with the utter fullness of God" (Ephesians 3:16-19).

Ways to Teach Prayer

There are, of course, numerous ways to help students encounter God in prayer. Perhaps some of the following suggestions will get you started.

Have a special prayer space. Though group prayer should never be forced, the prayer of routine has a real place too, before or after class or during a designated prayer period.

Choose a place, however small, in your teaching area and place symbols of prayer there, such as plants, candles, stones, a bowl of water, ashes, or shells. Always regard this place as one of quiet, and use it only for times of reflection and prayer.

Invite students to pray in silence. "Be still and know that I am God" is an excellent theme for prayer. Prayer is listening to God speaking to us. Encourage students to relax, sitting on the floor in your prayer space, breathing slowly and allowing the tensions of the day to slip away. Yoga breathing and yoga positions might be helpful. A tai-chi movement might help them center their breathing. Background music helps create a peaceful atmosphere.

To assist relaxation, lead a simple nature prayer using an object from nature: a stone, a sea shell, a branch, or a leaf. Invite students to talk to God about this object.

Pray in thanksgiving. Give each member of the group a piece of blank paper and have each write on the top "Thanks, God, for _____." Have them fold the paper into four squares. In each of the squares they can record their responses to these four aspects of their lives as a cause for thanksgiving. 1) A significant event that has happened recently, 2) A person who means a great deal to them at this moment, 3) Gifts or talents they have recently developed, 4) A place where they have discovered God this week. Gather all the sheets and place them in your prayer space where all these prayers will be an expression of ongoing thanks from your group.

Pray with the newspaper. To pray is to see God in the everyday events of life. "Newspaper" prayer is done by giving members of the group a page of newspaper and inviting them to select an item, for example, a news report, an advertisement, or a birth notice. Have them compose a prayer from this item. The newspaper can be their daily prayer book. Such prayer recalls God's presence in daily happenings.

Encourage journal writing. Have participants obtain a notebook. Each night or at least a few times a week, ask them to record their feelings and insights about what has been happening in their lives. These journals should be personal and private records of God's presence. Writing down some of the movements of the Spirit might help students see a kind of rhythm and pattern in their lives.

Prayer of Imagination

Active imagination is a power we possess to enter another place and time and recreate images. Through our imagination, we become the members of a crowd, disciples of Jesus, observers on the way to Calvary. We see, hear, smell, and experience entire scenes with our imaginations. Consider the following example.

Dramatically read this passage from Luke 7:11-17 to your students:

> It happened that soon afterwards he went to a town called Nain, accompanied by his disciples and a great number of people. Now when he was near the gate of the town there was a dead man being carried out, the only son of his mother, and she was a widow. A considerable number of the townspeople were with her. When the Lord saw her he felt sorry for her and said to her, "Don't cry." Then he went up and touched the bier and the bearers stood still, and he said, "Young man, I tell you: get up." And the dead man sat up and began to talk, and Jesus gave him to his mother. Everyone was filled with awe and glorified God saying, "A great prophet has risen up among us; we have been visited by God."

After some moments of quiet relaxation, invite participants to go back in time and place to become one of the followers of Jesus walking along the dusty roads of Palestine approaching the gates of Nain. They see the funeral procession winding its way toward them. The wailing of the women and the pain-filled face of the young man's mother give stark evidence of the grief and sense of hopelessness she is feeling. She is now completely alone. And so the dramatic events unfold.

After the initial "locating the scene" stage, read the passage again very slowly, pausing after each movement in the story, allowing the active imaginations of the group to transport them to this moving scene. Allow time for students to savor the images, and let these images evoke emotions in them.

A second way to involve students in prayer of imagination is to have them imagine themselves sitting on a chair in a bare room facing an empty chair. In their imaginations, the door opens and Jesus enters to take his place on the chair. After some time of quiet in his presence, invite them to dialogue with Jesus.

An alternate form of this method is to pray with images. Sometimes students pray best using images of God. In the bible God is described in many images, for example, as a rock, bread, shepherd, light, potter, and eagle. Also suggest a few non-biblical images, for example "God is like a tree, a cloud, a rainbow, a river, or a storm."

Encourage the group to use their active imaginations to allow God-images to emerge from their unconscious.

Learn Formula Prayers

Write the words of various prayers on an overhead, chart, or blackboard. In small groups, study each line or phrase of the prayers. Then present the ideas back to the main group. Consider the words of the Our Father, for example.

Our Father: Abba is perhaps the most revolutionary word spoken by Jesus. "Our" is a God for everyone, not exclusive to any one group. Calling God Father invites us to be children of trust. God is our provider and parent.

who art in heaven: God is bigger than our little world and God calls us beyond our everyday limits to eternal values.

hallowed be thy name: God's presence evokes a sense of wonder and awe. God is holy. Let us reverence God.

Your kingdom come: We long for the dream of God to create a new world where gospel values reign.

Your will be done on Earth: God wishes us to live in harmony with God's will.

as it is in heaven: Those who know God are fully in accord with God's loving plan for them.

Give us this day our daily bread: We beg God for what is needed to live each day: food, drink, love, challenge, and community. May all people experience this fulfillment.

and forgive us our trespasses as we forgive those who trespass against us: We ask for reconciliation with God as we forgive those who sin against us.

and lead us not into temptation, but deliver us from evil: We ask that evil may not overwhelm us and that we be saved from it. May God shepherd us always.

Techniques such as this help students appreciate the rich heritage of formula prayers which have helped Christians pray throughout the 2000 years of the Christian story.

Devotional Prayers

Try various devotional prayers. Explain the historical perspective of popular devotional forms, for example, devotion to the Sacred Heart.

Christians were inspired by the heart of Jesus pierced by a soldier's spear (John 19:32). Devotion to the loving heart of Jesus became popular in the Middle Ages. This devotion received a boost with the apparitions to St. Margaret Mary Alacoque at Paray-le-Monial in the 1670s. The contemporary symbols of this devotion come from these apparitions. Perhaps in our era of open heart surgery, there may be a need for new symbols to express the special love Jesus has for us.

The Rosary has been a popular Marian devotion. The history of the rosary offers many insights as to how a devotion changes in different eras of the church. In the Middle Ages the 150 Hail Marys with Our Fathers were said to match the 150 psalms said by the monks. Most people could not read the psalms. A popular title for Mary was "Rose" in this era so the prayer form gradually became known as the Rosary. Popular tradition tells how Dominic evidently used a form of the Rosary in his struggles against the Albigensians. The Albigensians emphasized the soul as the spirit trapped in a body. Matter was evil for them. The Rosary centers on the life of Jesus and Mary, and then the story of the incarnation sanctifies us in our humanity.

The rosary became a much more universal devotion after the battle of Lepanto in 1571, and the Feast of the Rosary (October 7th) was introduced at that time.

Pray with the psalms. These have been a traditional form of prayer in the Judaeo-Christian spiritual heritage. There are many ways of using them, for example: saying them, chanting or singing them, composing a modern version of one of the psalms, or making a collage based on the words of a psalm.

Teach Mary's prayer. The Magnificat from Luke 1:46-55 is a prayer for all Christians. It may be studied, sung, said, and then rewritten in a simple personal way, for example:

My whole being praises God my Savior,
because God has given me so many blessings
God cares so much for the little ones of the world.
The people who are proud will be challenged.
God is always merciful.
Long ago God made promises to Abraham and his people.
Ours is a faithful God who does not forget promises.

Chant scripture quotes as prayer. Do this slowly, just as a mantra is prayed. Consider these quotes: Set your hearts on his kingdom (Luke 12:31). Why are you so frightened? (Mark 4:40). Let your will be done, not mine (Luke 22:42). I have faith. Help my lack of faith (Mark 9:24).

Centering Prayer

Centering prayer is a type of prayer that helps us to enter the inner quiet of our being to discover God. It is like allowing a bucket to drop down the well of our inner selves to draw from the waters of God's gracious love. Centering prayer assists us to descend to the core of our being which is the "image of God" point.

For centering prayer, direct students to find a quiet place. Ask them to relax and develop a rhythm in their breathing. Then they should select a favorite phrase, word, or mantra, such as *Abba;* Jesus is Lord; My Lord and my God; God is love; Come, Holy Spirit; or Come, Lord Jesus.

Ask them to whisper or say the word or phrase until it becomes merged into their breathing. Then have them cease saying the word and allow God's presence to fill their being. Finally, invite them to slowly come back to their present place and awareness, and thank God for being present within them.

In *The Divine Milieu* Teilhard de Chardin described centering prayer this way: "I took the lamp, and leaving the zone of everyday occupations and relationship where everything seems clear, I went down into my innermost self."

Keep in mind that this approach may not appeal to everyone. There is a definite link between prayer and personality. God speaks to us through daily events and our own personalities. From personality indicators such as Myers-Briggs or the Enneagram, we learn that we have different ways of relating to our environment and different ways of perceiving. Each person's relationship with God is influenced by the ways they react with their world. Because students are uniquely different, a prayer program should cater to a wide diversity of prayer styles and approaches. Try to be sensitive to the needs of all.

Other Ways to Pray

Invite students to compose a personal prayer credo in which they state their key beliefs and express their faith in God. These credos should reflect the values they hope to live by. Encourage them to recite these daily.

Use ecumenical prayers. Research the various prayer forms and practices of other religious traditions such as Native American, Buddhist, Hindu, Jewish, and Islamic.

Change postures during prayer. Research the various postures of prayer. What have been the prayer postures of religious people through the ages? Which posture do your students prefer in prayer? Why? What are the main postures of people in prayer in different religious traditions? Once you have found answers, experiment with as many postures as possible.

Use blessings. Compose blessing services for your students, from you to them and from them to one another. Through blessings we acknowledge the giftedness of God in all that we have and are. Blessings help us to appreciate everything we have as a gift from God, and they celebrate this in word and gesture.

Study the prayer of Jesus. Search the gospels for the prayers of Jesus and his teachings on prayer. Here are several examples: Our Father: Matthew 6:5-13, Baptism of Jesus: Luke 3:21-22, Jesus in a lonely place: Mark 1:35, Choosing the twelve: Luke 6:12, Feeding the crowds: Luke 9:16, The transfiguration: Luke 9:29, Praising God: John 17:1-3, Jesus teaches about prayer: Luke 11:1-13, Last Supper prayer: Luke 22:17, Prayer for Simon: Luke 22:32, Agony in the garden: Luke 22:40, Prayer of self-giving: Luke 23:46, Prayer of missioning: Matthew 28:19-20.

When, where, and how did Jesus pray? Jesus was a devout Jew. What were the prayer practices and traditions of his time? How did Jesus exercise his ministry through prayer and worship? Share these questions and their answers with your students.

Liturgy and the Church Year

Celebrate with liturgy and prayer services. All religious traditions have some public and communal expressions of worship. Liturgy is the official prayer of the Christian community. It celebrates God's presence among people. The quality of the liturgy reflects the vitality or apathy of the Christian group. After the 6th century, liturgy tended to become more and more centered on the priest rather than the community. By the Middle Ages, the community was reduced to passivity, like spectators at a mysterious ritual in which they did not participate. After the Council of Trent, much attention was given to rubrics in liturgy, which confirmed that the "real" action of the liturgy was done by the priest and not the community.

The *Constitution on the Liturgy*, which was proclaimed on December 4, 1963, was one of the key documents of Vatican Council II in renewing the liturgy.

The seasons of the church year offer a cycle of movements through the passages of our life journeys: the waiting of Advent, the birth of the child of Christmas, the *metanoia* of Lent, the trauma of Calvary, the hope of Easter and the choice of life through the Spirit at Pentecost. The following suggestions might help you and your students celebrate the church year.

Advent and Christmas

"Plant" an Advent tree. Place a strong branch in some kind of pot or bucket with sand and decorate it. Scripture quotations can be hung from it as well as Advent promises.

Practice waiting. Invite your group to share experiences of waiting in their lives and discuss them, for example: waiting for a train or bus, waiting for a visitor, waiting for news from a friend, waiting to get better, or waiting for exam results.

Ask: How did you feel? Was your waiting worthwhile?

Make an Advent calendar. On a large piece of cardboard, mark off squares for each day of Advent. On pieces of paper, write a prayer, verse of scripture, suggested good action, or the name of a person, and fold the papers and glue one to each of the Advent squares. Open one paper daily during Advent and do the action, say the prayer, pray for the person, etc.

Prepare slides and music. Invite students to prepare a slide series using contemporary images. Have them choose readings from scripture and Advent songs to accompany the slides.

Plan a toy collection. Toys that are no longer wanted in the home can be collected and given to charitable organizations such as St. Vincent de Paul or the Salvation Army for distribution to poor children before Christmas.

Write Christmas notes. Have students write "Merry Christmas" notes in as many languages as they can to remind people that the peace of Christ is for all nations. Some examples of "Merry Christmas" in other languages are: Italy: Buon Natale, Germany: Frohliche Weinachten, Holland: Zalig Kerstfeest, France: Joyeux Noel, and China: Kung Hsi Hsin Nien. You might also encourage your group to collect and share Christmas customs from other nations.

Choose a Kristkindl. Kristkindl is a German custom. Each person in the group puts her or his name on a slip of paper. The slips are put into a box and names are drawn. The name drawn is the Kristkindl person for Advent. Every day the person does something special for the Kristkindl partner without revealing his or her name. Each week, the person writes to the Kristkindl partner saying what he or she has done, and just before Christmas the identity of each Kristkindl is revealed.

Make a Jesse Tree. Again use a branch or draw a large paper tree. Make and decorate this tree with symbols of the ancestors of Jesus, for example: Adam (apple symbol), Noah (ark), Abraham (knife), Joseph (multi-colored coat), Moses (tablet), David (harp), and Solomon (temple).

Lent and Easter

The season of Lent developed from the Christian preparation for Easter. The forty days commemorate the forty days of Jesus in the desert. *Lentare* means springtime. Lent is the time to re-direct us to the centrality of Christ as savior.

Easter is *the* feast of the church year since it celebrates the resurrection of Jesus. Easter empowers all Christians to cry "Alleluia is our song."

Lenten themes are: seeing clearly and conversion; baptism and the catechumenate; failure as a new beginning; healing, fasting, and penance; mysteries of the death and resurrection; sacrifice as self-giving; conversion to the way of discipleship; and sorrow and reconciliation.

Try the following teaching approaches.

Celebrate an Ash Wednesday paraliturgy with each person bringing some leaves representing something they wish to let go of in their lives. Place the leaves in a metal wastebasket and burn them. Then using the ashes, have each person in the group sign the forehead of the person next to her or him saying, "May Jesus take away your sins." Then invite the group to express sorrow for their sins in song and prayer.

As a class, support Operation Rice Bowl all during Lent.

Reflect on the Sunday gospels together.

Enact the Way of the Cross. The stations may be the traditional ones or may be adapted to your group. Your stations might include: the Last Supper, arrest of Jesus, Jesus being condemned, Jesus carrying his cross, Jesus meeting his mother, Jesus falling three times, Jesus being helped by Simon, Jesus meeting the weeping women, Jesus being crucified, and Jesus speaking from the cross, Jesus dying, Jesus being taken from the cross, Jesus being raised from the dead.

Have your group study baptism during Lent and have a recommitment to baptism during a ceremony toward the end of the season, perhaps during Holy Week.

Study the cycle of life and death in nature. Invite students to give examples of the cycle and if possible illustrate them with pictures and samples to show how the death and life cycle continues throughout the world.

Study various kinds of cross symbols which illustrate how the mystery of paradox is expressed. The symbol of the cross helps us to appreciate the role of suffering in human life. Your class might discuss the place of suffering in human life, and how suffering can lead to growth and change. Then research the history of fasting and penance in the Christian church. What is the purpose of fasting in Christian discipleship? Invite discussion of this.

Prepare symbols of Lent and Easter, such as eggs, cross, light, path, and the sun.

Prepare and celebrate a Seder meal. This is an adaptation of the Jewish passover meal. Its purpose is to recall the events of the Exodus and to thank God for the call to freedom. Those participating in a Seder meal need to be sensitive to the sacredness of the Jewish passover meal and not in any sense attempt to "Christianize" the Jewish ritual.

Easter Symbols

Make special use of Easter symbols such as the following:

The sun. People sometimes gather at sunrise on Easter Sunday because the risen Christ is symbolized by the rising sun.

The butterfly reminds us of the risen Christ who came out of his tomb. The caterpillar wraps itself in a cocoon and breaks out to become a butterfly.

"Alleluia," a special prayer for Easter. It comes from two Hebrew words *hallel*, an expression of praise, and *Jahve*, God's name. So alleluia means "Praise God."

The egg is a symbol of the tomb of Jesus. The chicken breaks out of the shell, just as Jesus broke out of the tomb of death. Easter eggs are colored and painted with Easter symbols and given as gifts. This is a German custom from the Middle Ages.

The lily. In the northern hemisphere, Easter and spring coincide. The lily symbolizes all spring flowers that burst forth in color.

An Easter parade. Our parades today have been adapted from the old church practice of religious processions in which people walked together and stopped to pray at certain places.

Research the origins of Easter with your students. The feast of Easter was the only liturgical Sunday feast for the first three centuries of Christianity. It dates from the Council of Nicaea in 325 C.E. when the church Fathers declared that Easter would be observed on the first Sunday following the first full moon after March 21.

The Solemnity of Pentecost

The feast of Pentecost celebrates the coming of the Spirit to the followers of Jesus (Acts 2). It is the birthday of the church. The Jewish people celebrate the Feast of Weeks (or Pentecost) 50 days after Passover. The synagogue is decorated with harvest festival symbols such as plants, wheat, and flowers.

The three special symbols of the Christian Pentecost, fire, wind, and tongues, are images of God's transforming power in the Hebrew Scriptures. The wind of God is a creative force in the world (Genesis 1:2; Ezekiel 37:1-10; Genesis 8:1); fire is a sign of God's presence (Exodus 3:1-6); tongues suggest that the Tower of Babel is reversed because the Spirit enables all people to communicate through the name of Jesus (Genesis 11:1-9).

Try these Pentecost activities.

Discuss with your students each of the seven gifts of the Spirit and their effect on our Christian lives: wisdom, understanding, knowledge, piety, courage, reverence, and wonder.

Say a prayer to the Holy Spirit in every class, for example: "Come Holy Spirit, fill the hearts of the faithful. Kindle in us the fire of your love and renew the face of the earth."

Research the history of confirmation. What is its relationship to baptism?

Study the gospels (especially the Gospel of Luke) and list the references to the Holy Spirit. Have students each choose a favorite passage and use it as the basis for a prayer to the Holy Spirit.

The Eucharistic Liturgy

The eucharist is the central act of celebration for all Christians and the church's greatest prayer. In preparing for liturgy in school or parish programs, the following considerations should be observed: The theme for the Mass should be appropriate for the group and the liturgical church season. Where possible the group should be involved in the preparation. There must be a certain flow to liturgy so that it does not appear as a series of creative events. A sense of mystery should be observed. The celebrant needs to be involved in the preparation and comfortable with what is proposed. The physical environment should be comfortable and aesthetically pleasant with banners, symbols, and appropriate music.

Prayer Services

Christian communities engage in prayer services as well as through the official liturgy. Prayer services are not prescriptive in form or ritual. They may develop spontaneously from a group or be planned through a reflection on appropriate symbols, readings, and music from a theme chosen for the service.

Prayer services are today becoming an important element in worship forms of the Christian community. As the difficulty of obtaining the services of priests increases and also the awareness of how the people of God exercise their baptismal call develops, more varied forms of worship are being used. Some key elements of a prayer service are: introduction, songs, readings, reflections, symbols, group expressions, movement, dance, or symbolic gestures, and a conclusion. A special form of a prayer service is a blessing ritual. Prayers of blessings affirm our giftedness and God's love for us. Use blessing gestures such as placing hands on heads, linking arms, and the use of holy water.

Conclusion

Religion teachers have many opportunities to pray with those they teach. But they are primarily witnesses to prayer and should be nurturing their own prayer life. The depth and authenticity of their relationships with God will be their first affirmation and greatest lesson about prayer.

Ways to Respond

•Make a list of all the ways that you presently pray with your students. Beside each item, describe how effective it is.

•Ask your students how they would *like* to pray. Are there prayer forms they want to know more about? Encourage them to research these forms and share them with the total group.

•Spend time analyzing how you pray personally. Try to set aside time each day and try various prayer forms until you find one that best helps you communicate with God.

Questions for Reflection and/or Discussion

•Do you set aside time for prayer every time you teach? Why or why not?

•Do you consider prayer moments time well spent? What responses from students suggest this to you?

•Do you ever use prayer of imagination with those you teach? Have you ever participated in this type of prayer?

•What is your favorite form for personal prayer? When do you practice it?

•What prayer experiences have worked best in your classes? How have your students reacted to them?

•What new prayer forms are you willing to try in future classes?

Notes

Teaching about
the Church

The word "church" evokes many diverse images, for example, a building, priest or minister, community, family, obligations, Mass, serving the poor, or parish. Throughout the two thousand years of Christian history, there have been many images of church, including the following: vine and branches (John 15:1-5), sheepfold with the Good Shepherd as leader (John 10:11), Body of Christ (1 Corinthians 10:16-17), The Way (Acts of the Apostles), one true church of Christ (Council of Trent), Mystical Body of Christ (Pope Pius XII, 1943), Pilgrim people (Constitution of the Church), People of God (Constitution on the Church), and Servant (Constitution on the Church in the Modern World).

The various theologies for church have been shaped by cultural and historical contexts. The "one true church" image was popular at a time of serious religious divisions during the Reformation era; the "servant" image of the church is more popular in countries in which the majority of the population live in dire poverty and under oppressive political systems. When the papacy was threatened by the invasion of the papal states, the doctrine of papal infallibility was defined. Though it is the one church of Jesus, the church will always be interpreted by specific cultures. It is only in this way that its mission and identity will be appropriate for each specific society.

The Meaning of Church

The word "church," from the Greek *ekklesia*, originally referred to a public assembly for political purposes. *Ekklesia* means a people who are "called out" to a meeting by a herald. This concept of church suited the early Christians who felt that they were called or chosen by God. Scripture scholars debate whether Jesus actually founded a church. What we are certain of is that he preached the reign of God and gathered a community of disciples to announce the good news of salvation. The church is a community of disciples who live, celebrate, proclaim the glad tidings of salvation in Jesus, and work to enhance the well being of humankind. The church is a pilgrim people who are missioned through the power of the Spirit to share the dream of Jesus for the transformation of the world.

The nature of the church is rooted in the mystery of the Trinity. God as Father and Mother is love. Love generates life in the Son who reveals God's love. The Spirit generates life in us to become children of God and draws us into union with the source of our being. The church intends to express the dynamic relationships of the Trinity as community. The diversity of the community is drawn together into unity through the energy of love.

As we have already said, the mission of the church is described in the New Testament as *diakonia:* service to the world, *kerygma:* evangelizing and teaching, *koinonia:* living the community of disciples, and *leiturgia:* worship and spirituality.

Church Structures

The vision and values of the kingdom of God are the essence of the church. Church organization has its reference point in fidelity to the values of the reign of God as proclaimed by Jesus. The only "structure" initiated by Jesus was the institution of the twelve, and this structure disappeared after the death of Stephen. Although there was no uniform church institution in the New Testament, various elements of structures for pastoral ministry were clearly in evidence in such early church documents as the Pastoral Epistles, the *Didache,* and the writings of Clement of Rome, Ignatius of Antioch, and Irenaeus.

By the beginning of the second century, more regular pastoral structures were evident. The local churches were led by an *episkopos* (supervisor) who was assisted by a group of elders *(presbyteros).* The *episkopos* or bishop was the designated leader of the faith community, while the presbyters constituted a group of advisors. Later in the fourth century, the priesthood emerged from the office of the presbyter. Ministry was a service to the community and the whole community was involved in decision making. The task of leadership ministry was to encourage the expression of the variety of ministries within the church as a service for the world. The power of Christian leadership is to empower others to realize their gifts of the Spirit.

The concept of apostolic succession was an important element in the evolution of church order. Apostolic succession was the belief that those who held authoritative leadership in the church were linked with the commission of the apostles and were entrusted with the task of maintaining the original ministry of the church.

The New Testament records the pre-eminence of the leadership role of Peter. The Petrine ministry became a significant feature of church life in early Christian times. There has been considerable debate about what has been constituted in church structures by divine ordinance and what has been established by ecclesiastical direction, and about which structures may be modified at the discretion of the church community. What is clear is that the office and structures of the church must always be a service to the mission of the church. The church's mission is an extension of the ministry of Jesus and the energizing influence of the Holy Spirit.

Three Eras in the Church Story

Culturally, the church has experienced three eras. The first era lasted officially until the first Council of Jerusalem in 49 C.E. when Paul was able to win the day against those who taught that people could become Christians only through the Jewish rituals and practices. As the center of Christian authority shifted from Jerusalem to Rome, Christianity became more identified with Roman and Greek culture.

In this second era, which lasted until the 1960s, European cultural norms became the basis for liturgy, catechetics, philosophy, and theology.

After the Second World War, the rapid expansion of the churches in Africa, Oceania, and South America brought new dimensions to the face of the Catholic church. It became truly a universal church rather than a Roman church. By 1980, the majority of Catholics in the world were poor, even desperately poor. During the 1970s the issue of inculturation became a pivotal one as Christian communities sought to interact with their local cultures rather than accept a European and foreign way of being

Christian. Belonging to a centralized universal church and yet establishing a clear local identity is not an easy task for church leaders, especially in cultures that are not European in origin.

New Theologies

One consequence of the church becoming a world church was the emergence of new theologies that reflected "faith seeking understanding." Such theologies sought to articulate a faith response to the real needs of people.

Three significant theologies that represent creative responses to the cultural environment are liberation theology, feminist theology, and creation theology. Since the majority of Catholics are poor and oppressed, liberation theology seeks a transformation in the political and economic spheres through which everyone can experience basic human rights.

Feminist theology explores our understanding of the creative partnership between women and men, as opposed to the dominance of patriarchy. Feminist theology critiques the value systems within the church and society and exposes some of the idolatrous assumptions about how God is perceived and the kind of human order that has been sanctified by church practice and law.

Creation theology is a response to the ecological crisis. It recalls and renames the original covenant between God, us, and Earth. These theologies have enriched the mission and spirituality of the Christian community, which is always striving to interpret the Jesus event within a pluralism of cultures and political ideologies.

World Dialogue

The church is engaged in a dialogue with other religious traditions that do not have a Christian vision. Christians account for less than a quarter of the world's population and only very recently have acknowledged that the mystery of God's revelation to the majority of the world's population does not come through Christ. Today theologians of many religions search for an appreciation and understanding of the "God beyond all gods," the divine presence who is beyond all the various expressions of religious truth. In the face of ecological and military threats to our very existence, Christians are being challenged to listen to and celebrate the divine revelation in the various religious stories and traditions of the world. Perhaps the special role of the Christian church is to announce the faithful love of God in Jesus and to witness to this love through service and a reconciling community of life.

Models and Marks

The work of Avery Dulles in *Models of the Church* (see Suggested Resources) offered a useful paradigm that assisted us in an appreciation of the mystery of the church. His work has been further developed by other writers. Today the church is considered from several perspectives, for example: The church is an institution with organization, offices, and pastoral structures.

It is a community of disciples, a community who seeks to live out the ideals of the invitation of Jesus to discipleship. The church is a sign that gives witness to the transcendent Spirit in the world and the quest for holiness. It is prophetic, especially when the people of God speak out against oppression. The church is a servant, committed to serving the world, especially the marginalized. It is an evangelist because the role of the church is to announce the good news of Jesus.

Because the institutional model of the church has been so dominant since the Middle Ages, there is a sharp reaction to its authority and bureaucracy in western contemporary consciousness. The emphasis on the juridicial and authority elements of church life evolved as a result of its cultural association with the Roman Empire and its reaction against the attacks of the Reformation churches. The Second Vatican Council was called to reconsider the role of the church in the world and to renew its spirit in accord with the gospels.

Another way of looking at the church is to return to the fourfold description formulated by the Council of Constantinople (381 C.E.). This formulation is included in the words of the Nicene creed. The church is described as: "one, holy, catholic, and apostolic." Each of these "marks" of the church denotes a particular characteristic: One, the unity of the church, suggests a common belief and worship. Holy means that the community seeks to be faithful to God's invitation to love more fully. Catholic means the church is for all people in every culture. Apostolic means that the church continues its ministry from Jesus and apostolic times.

Contemporary Issues

There are many issues facing the church today, including all of the following:

Justice: An even greater commitment to justice questions is needed to work toward a more humane society and better quality of life. The number of people living in debilitating situations is intolerable and incidences of violence, homelessness, alienation, and poverty are growing.

Ecology: The future of our planet will depend on every significant world agency cooperating to save Earth. The church has enormous resources to support governments and other community groups to care for Earth and its resources.

Revisiting the kingdom story: The values and vision of Jesus and the reign of God must be the foundational stance of the church in a critique of its institutions and pastoral practices. The church must examine carefully whether power is exercised to set free the energies of the Spirit or is being employed to manipulate and oppress people.

Spirituality: The church needs to make accessible to its people spiritualities that touch the realities of ordinary life. In the face of secular materialism, the quest for appropriate spiritualities is an imperative one.

Leadership: Collaborative styles of leadership that are congruent with our gospel heritage and our appreciation of Christian leadership should be the norm of church leadership.

Ministry: An awareness of ministry and formation for ministries will channel the gifts of the community toward the mission of the church. In the past, the church's limited view of ministry weakened the effectiveness of its evangelization and service.

Women in partnership: The incorporation of women into the life of the church at all levels will greatly enrich the community.

Pastoral planning: Through effective pastoral planning the resources of the community would be more wisely used and appropriate structural changes be made.

Adult faith education: Planning for a "birth-to-death" faith education will ensure that adults are motivated and assisted to participate in the faith education of their children.

Ecumenism: A vigorous pursuit of unity among the diversity of religious traditions will help all of us better acknowledge the presence of God in our lives and affirm the sacredness of all human life.

Local churches in unity: The movement from a highly centralized church to a communion of local churches with a unifying focus will enable all churches to be responsible for their destinies and leadership.

Celebrating church: In an age of pessimism and anxiety, the church can be a sign of hope and resurrection.

Evangelization: The very nature of the church is to evangelize, to announce the good news using available media technology.

These issues are neither exhaustive nor comprehensive. However, they are offered to provoke thinking about how the church might better fulfill its essential mission. If it is orientated toward its mission, it will remember its past while shaping its future. The church's history and structures will not become oppressive baggage but rather signposts along the way.

As a way of summing up, I would like to share with you what I see as the goals of the church in its mission to the world today. I will list these as a prayer. I invite you to pray it often—with and for the church.

Jesus, you have called us to be church. May we always give witness to the mystery of the Trinity through vital Christian communities in which love is our bond.

May we deepen the heritage of our Christian traditions and more fully receive God's revelation.

Help us to affirm the dignity of humankind, to reveal and live out the good news of the reign of God, and to strive for holiness.

Give us the courage to work toward a more just society by supporting agencies that enhance the quality of life, and show us how to care for Earth in all that we do.

May we be prophets of hope to those in despair by making your resurrection known.

May we witness to our belief in the partnership of men and women, and fully respect all peoples everywhere. Amen.

The goals in this prayer offer a charter for pastoral planners in dioceses and parishes. Though they are broad and far-reaching, we can draw much consolation from the parting message of Jesus: "And know that I am with you always, yes, to the end of time" (Matthew 28:20).

Conclusion

The doctrine of the "communion of saints" teaches us about the sacred community of all those who are united with us in Christian fellowship: Mary, the saints in heaven, and all of us here on Earth. The church is a messy mixture of saints and sinners, poets, artists, musicians, academics, unlettered people, clergy, explorers, scientists, skeptics, healers, and people from every possible profession.

To be a member of the church is to join the pilgrim journeys of many ordinary Christians who are struggling to understand life and faith and God's presence in their lives.

Ways to Respond

•Discuss your understanding of church with other catechists and teachers using these models: community, sign, servant, prophet, institution, and herald. Before the discussion, write down beside each term 1) what you think it means, and 2) if you have seen any evidence of it in action.

•Research the history of your local parish with those you teach, and then discuss how it is responding to its mission now.

•Reflect on these challenging issues facing the church today: ministry, women and church, media and the church, inculturation, evangelization, secularism, and spirituality. Which issue seems most pressing to you?

Questions for Reflection and/or Discussion

•What do you think of the goals for the church listed in this chapter? What goals would you add?

•What is your personal reaction to these statements?:

I don't understand what's happening in the church anymore. It's changed so much.

I find it hard to relate to a church that treats women like second-class citizens.

What I like about the church is its clear authoritative teaching. I don't need the church to help me get in touch with spiritual things.

It disturbs me to see the church losing so many of its members, especially the young.

•What is your dream for the church? How should it be structured? What would you like to see happen to people in your parish?

Notes

Chapter 9

Teaching about
Sacraments and Sacramentality

A quiet revolution is happening in our understanding of sacraments and sacramentality. Since the Middle Ages and until recently there had been an emphasis on the form and matter of the sacraments. Sacraments were things to be received to gain grace. People went to sacraments to get more grace. This "banking" theory tended to view sacraments as seven deposits of grace to which people came for spiritual benefits. Certain conditions pertained to the reception of each sacrament.

The role of the priest was a central one in dispensing the sacraments. Because of the Protestant attacks on some of the sacramental practices of the Catholic church, the Council of Trent stressed clear definitions that performed a service in clarifying essential doctrines of the sacraments. However, it neglected the role of the Christian community and the mystery of encountering Jesus. In more recent times sacramental theology has undergone many developments. Some of the more significant ones follow.

1. Sacraments are not sacred rites that come from God to our secular world but rather profound symbols of God's living presence *in our world.* The bread of the eucharist is also about the hungers of the world. The initiation of baptism to God's family is a challenge to racism.

Hence the idea of sacramentality needs to be understood as a context for sacraments. Sacraments are not divorced from life; they make life holy. Sacramentality is the awareness and celebration of God in the world.

2. The sacraments are not individual acts of piety but expressions of God's saving love within the context of the Christian community. The emphasis in baptism is not on ensuring the baby's passage to heaven but the initiation into the Christian community as a child of God. The community celebrates the sacraments rather than receives them. Sacraments are not so much for individual salvation but *community* celebrations of God's gracious love through Jesus.

3. The original word in the New Testament was *mysterion* or "mystery" but was translated to *sacramentum,* or "sacrament," meaning a kind of pledge or consecration. In Mark 4:11 Jesus says to the disciples, "To you has been given the *mysterion* of the kingdom of God." *Mysterion* implies a mystery of relationships within a human community and that sacraments do not belong to the church alone, but are occasions for God's mercy and love to be proclaimed to the whole world. The sacraments stand firmly on God's creation of the world and cannot be the exclusive domain of any one group of peo-

ple. They are pathways to enter the mysteries of the universe with its cycle of life and death. Sacraments are faith expressions of God's presence in every movement of creation.

4. There is a growing awareness of the integral relationship between sacrament and Word. After the reformation, Protestants tended to emphasize the Word of God and minimize sacramental rituals, while Catholics tended to do the reverse. In more recent times, ecumenical dialogue has closed this gap. Catholics are engaged in scripture studies and give more attention to the proclamation of the Word within sacramental liturgies.

5. There has been a movement from a preoccupation with form and substance to an awareness of relationships within the sacramental experience. The emphasis has shifted from concerns about the size of the host, how long the presence of Jesus stays with us after communion, the hand or the tongue for the reception of communion, to an awareness of the loving presence of Jesus in the Christian community.

6. Sacraments are intended to express themes of the kingdom of God. The kingdom themes of new relationships, conversion, commitment, suffering being transformed, and action for justice are integral to the celebration of the sacraments.

7. Sacraments must flow into the life of the community and the world. Baptism into the community challenges the pain of racism and our desire to belong, the bread of eucharist jolts us into listening to cries for food, especially from the starving. Sacraments cannot be divorced from a quest for justice and transformation.

8. The ecumenical dialogue on sacraments has been very fruitful. There is now a growing consensus among Christians about many aspects of the theology of the sacraments. Catholic thinking has been influenced by the context of the sacrament within the Christian community, while the Protestants have been more open to the significance of ritual and symbol.

Today we have expanded our understanding of the sacraments by studying their historical evolution, as well as by our awareness of human development and our knowledge of other religious traditions. Immediately following the Second Vatican Council, the church sought to revitalize sacramental rites and liturgy. However, urgent guidelines are still needed to respond to such questions as: Should infant baptism be continued? Do we continue to have confirmation as a separate sacrament? and Should there be more than seven sacraments?

Teaching about Sacramentality

An understanding of sacramentality is basic to effective teaching of sacraments. By sacramentality we mean an awareness of God in our lives and in nature. The sense of awe and wonder, such as experiences of watching the face of a newborn child, a sunset, a rainbow, a satellite moving through the firmament, are events or occasions that evoke wonder and awe. God's mysterious creative power is everywhere, if only we observe with a listening heart. Sacramentality helps us enter the *mysterion* of God's love through the world of creation.

Following are some suggested ways to teach about sacramentality.

Reflect with students on poems that evoke images of the divine presence throughout creation. This ancient Zen saying, for example, expresses the need for stillness so that beauty can touch us.

In spring, hundreds of flowers,
in autumn a harvest moon;
in summer a refreshing breeze;
in winter snow will accompany you.
If useless things do not hang in your mind,
any season is a good season for you.

Play music for your students. Encourage them to take a very relaxed position. Allow the music to enter their souls. These examples of music may help evoke a sense of beauty and peace: Beethoven's Pastoral Symphony and

Ode to Joy from the Ninth Symphony, James Galway's Songs of the Seashore, and the theme song from Chariots of Fire.

Take a group to a field and allot each person a "plot" or section. Each should study his or her plot carefully, noting the texture of the grass, the soil, any living things such as worms, and seek to become "one" with their plot. Students should then gather and share observations about what their plots contain.

Give each student a nature object, such as a branch, stone, or flower. Have them study the nature object, feel it, smell it, observe it, and then with closed eyes allow the shape and texture to become part of them.

Help each person in the group to explore parts of his or her body, such as the eyes, ears, feet, and hands. This gentle exploration helps us appreciate the gift of our bodies. Students may do such activities as: slow walks, rhythm breathing, a tai-chi movement, or a yoga position.

Ask students to recall some event that was a deep experience for them, such as: seeing a new baby, a journey to a mountain, watching the sea break on rocks, swimming underneath a waterfall, or visiting a dying relative in the hospital. Then discuss: Why did this event touch you so profoundly?

Ask students to reflect on some apparently "ordinary" event, pausing to allow the event to become an enriched experience by bringing it into consciousness. How did they feel? What happened? Who was involved? Why did the event touch them?

Sacraments are special meeting times with God in Jesus within the context of the Christian community. Sacrament times are passage times that mark beginnings, reconcilings, celebrating, and choices on the life journey.

To appreciate sacraments as encounters with the Lord, have your group discuss encounters with people that have been particularly meaningful. Then ask: When does a meeting with another become significant? How do we encounter Jesus? Then meditate on these scripture passages in which Jesus met people: Luke 18:35-43 (blind man of Jericho), Luke 7:36-50 (woman at Simon's house), Luke 7:11-17 (widow of Nain), Mark 7:31-37 (deaf man).

Sacraments express through sacred rituals the presence and ministry of Jesus. In this sense one may say that Jesus instituted the seven sacraments, although, of course the specific rituals and definition of the sacraments were not finalized until the Council of Trent. Sacraments celebrate the seasons of our lives.

Signs and Symbols

Signs are all around us. We can identify signs that tell us what to do, where to go, and at what speed to travel. Such signs have no meaning beyond the instruction they give. They might be called "direction" signs. Other signs have a deeper meaning, and they might be termed "effective" signs. They convey some special meaning through their actions. For example, a handshake conveys friendship and greeting; an invitation to a meal speaks of hospitality and welcoming; a birthday gift signifies friendship and remembering. Invite your students to identify some effective signs and then discuss them.

Symbols can never be completely described, but they do stimulate our imaginations and thought. We can never exhaust the meaning of symbols. Religious symbols point to ultimate realities. Symbols are culturally determined, but there are some that have an almost universal significance. These are called archetypal symbols, for example, a road, a tree, a mountain, a rock, or water.

Consider for example a tree, one of the most universal of all religious symbols. Some of the following images arise from the tree symbol: the three levels of life: The roots in the earth below symbolize our unconsciousness. The trunk stands for our present realities, and the leaves pointing to the sky symbolize our future. Trees contain the life cycle of the seasons, representing our own life cycles of summer, autumn, winter, and spring.

We are symbolic people by nature. The dream world is a language of symbols. Symbols arise in our unconscious and shape our conscious world. They affect our emotions as well as our intellect, and convey meaning about our reality. The church uses symbols to help us enter the mystery of God's presence.

In assisting your group to appreciate symbols, use the following ideas:

Invite students to discuss important family and personal symbols, for example, a vase, ring, table, or a photo.

Visit the church and research the symbols there: holy water, stations of the cross, sanctuary lamp, cross, images of Mary, flowers, altar, stained glass windows.

Take each of the symbols used in the sacramental rituals and research their significance: oil, water, light, bread, wine, rings, laying on of hands, salt, and names.

Compose symbols that would be appropriate for the marginalized, a peace group, an environment group, a Christian prayer gathering, the local school.

Research the use and significance of symbols in the various religious traditions.

The Place of Ritual

A ritual is a series of ordered actions. Every day we employ rituals in washing, shaving, greetings, birthdays, weddings, and meals. Secular rituals are part of everyday life. Religious rituals recall special events in the sacred history of the group. When the Jewish people escaped from Egypt and journeyed to Palestine, the event became ritualized in the annual passover meal. The passover meal in turn became ritualized by Christians in the eucharist.

These activities might help your students to better appreciate rituals.

Identify some everyday rituals.

Compose a ritual for celebrating the beginning or end of the school year.

Examine the sequence of actions in some national rituals, such as Thanksgiving Day, the Fourth of July, Mother's Day, or Father's Day.

Research various sacred rituals in different religious traditions, for example, the initiation

rituals of Native Americans.

Develop a religious ritual for a recommitment to baptism.

A key concept in understanding sacraments is the idea of "liminality," which is taken from the writings of the anthropologist Turner in his book *The Ritual Process* (see Suggested Resources). Turner sees a three-phase movement in how people may grow into a new consciousness. Applying this to the Christian journey, the stages would be:

1. *Separation:* the person or group moves away from the ordinary life situation.

2. *Liminality:* the person or group is confronted with basic human and spiritual values without the normal cultural and personal supports. He or she is invited to a deep conversion of personal commitment.

3. *Aggregation:* the person merges again with the wider group, the Christian community, and then the societal environment with a new enrichment from the liminality experience.

In the sacraments, the participant moves from the ordinary day routine (separation), enters into an encounter with God's saving love in Jesus (liminality), and then returns to the Christian community and the ordinary social environment with a deepened experience of God's graciousness (aggregation).

Teaching Baptism

Baptism is the foundation sacrament. All Christian life begins at baptism whereby a person enters the Christian community as a disciple of Jesus. One of the clear directions in liturgical thinking today is to restore the earliest traditional practice of initiation into the body of Christ: baptism by water, confirmation by laying on of hands or anointing with oil, and eucharistic participation. The catechumenate (RCIA) has reclaimed this tradition for adults but there are certain pastoral difficulties associated with infant baptism that are unresolved in our current church.

Use the following ideas to share the meaning of baptism with your students. Consider the various kinds of beginnings that occur in your lives. How do people react to beginnings? What rituals do they use? What is left behind? What hopes or anxieties?

Study initiation rites in clubs, religious groups, and mythology. Extract from the different examples some common elements of initiation.

Discuss how we can be incorporated into groups. What needs to happen for such incorporation?

Witness a baptism and then research the use of symbols of water, light, names, oil, etc. Find examples of these symbols in the bible.

Research the catechumenate in the life of the church. Consider the significance of each of the stages of the initiation rite (RCIA): inquiry, catechumenate, enlightenment, and deepening of commitment (or mystagogia). What is the importance of the catechumenate in the church today?

Make a list of the names of each person in your group. Try to find the significance of these names in religious traditions. Which names are the names of canonized saints? Research the lives of these saints.

Write a story or play about the life of a Christian in the time of the Roman persecutions.

Reflect on the baptism of Jesus, according to Mark 1:9-11.

It was at this time that Jesus came from Nazareth in Galilee and was baptized in the Jordan by John. No sooner had he come up out of the water than he saw the heavens torn apart and the Spirit, like a dove, descending on him. And a voice came from heaven, "You are my Son, the beloved; my favor rests on you."

Consider the images and symbols used in this description and then have the group prepare a baptism service in which there is a renewal of baptismal promises.

Baptism is the sacrament by which we are in-corporated into Christ's family. It is the beginning of a life journey for Christians and the commencement of a process of growth as God's sons and daughters.

Confirmation

Confirmation in current liturgical practice is a sacrament seeking an identity. Originally it was an integral element of the initiation rite, but it became separate after the fifth century. Various theologies were developed to rationalize its pastoral significance. Confirmation could be regarded as a rite of initiation, a sacrament of affirmation, or a sacrament of Christian commitment.

In the early church, *chrismation* (the anointing with consecrated oil), was the completion rite in the sacrament of baptism. It has been suggested that the name "consignation," which was used in the early church to describe the anointing, was derived from the theme of Paraclete or Advocate, which Jesus uses to describe the role of the Holy Spirit (John 14). The Spirit is described as the one who pleads for us, our counselor, our support, and advocate on the way. "Consignation" denotes one who signs up for us as a witness and support of our Christian endeavors. Confirmation is the sacrament in which the Spirit is invited to be within us to integrate our being with Christ. The fruits of the Spirit are the renewed presence of Jesus within us.

Use these ideas to teach the sacrament of confirmation:

Study the bible references to the *ruah*, the breath of God. In the creation story the breath of God is a life giving breath: "God's spirit hovered over the water" (Genesis 1:2); "Yahweh God fashioned man of dust from the soil, and then breathed into his nostrils a breath of life and thus man became a living being" (Genesis 2:7); "God sent a wind across the earth and the waters subsided" (Genesis 8:1); "The Lord Yahweh says this to these bones: 'I am going to make breath enter you and you will live'" (Ezekiel 37:5).

Consider Spirit symbols such as fire and

cloud: "There the angel of Yahweh appeared to him in the shape of a flame of fire, coming from the middle of a bush" (Exodus 3:2); "But for all this, you put not your faith in Yahweh your God who had gone in front of you on the journey to find you a camping ground, by night in the fire to light your path, by day in the cloud" (Deuteronomy 1:33).

Reflect on the Pentecost story from Acts 2:1-13. Note that at the coming of the Spirit the tower of Babel is reversed. People of diverse tongues are now able to communicate with each other through the power of the Spirit. The wind of the Spirit and the tongues of fire symbolize the presence of God.

Discuss personal experiences of life-giving and life-inhibiting times in your students' lives. How do they help others to become more alive? How do they put others down and inhibit life? Are they "life" people?

Research the gospels for mention of Jesus and the Holy Spirit, especially in the Gospel of Luke. For example: "While Jesus, after his own baptism, was at prayer, heaven opened and the Holy Spirit descended on him in bodily shape like a dove" (Luke 3:21-22); "Filled with the Holy Spirit, Jesus left the Jordan and was led by the Spirit through the wilderness"(Luke 4:1); "Jesus, with the power of the Spirit in him, returned to Galilee"(Luke 4:14).

Carefully read Luke 1:26-42, the story of the Annunciation, and share ideas about how Mary was a woman of the Spirit.

Identify some "Spirit" people throughout history. Why might they be called this? Whose lives did they touch?

Read Paul's description of gifts of the Spirit in 1 Corinthians 12:4-11 as follows:

There is a variety of gifts but always the same Spirit. There are many services to be done, but always to the same Lord; working in all sorts of different ways in different people, it is the same God who is working in all of them. The particular way in which the Spirit is given to each

person is for a good purpose. Some may have the gift of preaching with wisdom given them by the Spirit; others may have the gift of preaching instruction given them by the same Spirit; and still others the gift of faith given by the same Spirit; others again the gift of healing, through this one Spirit; one, the power of miracles; another, prophecy, another the gift of recognizing spirit; another the gift of tongues and another the ability to interpret them. All these are the work of one and the same Spirit who distributes different gifts to different people.

In Christian tradition, seven (a mystic number of wholeness) gifts of the Spirit have been identified. These are wisdom, knowledge, understanding, counsel, courage, piety, and awe of the Lord. Ask students to give examples of how these gifts of the Spirit might be expressed today. Then have them examine each of the symbols in the confirmation rite and research their meaning, including the laying on of hands, sign of the cross, anointing with oil, and being "sent out" and missioned. Be sure to identify for students the main movements in the confirmation rite.

Teaching Eucharist

The word "eucharist" means thanksgiving. The eucharist is the summit of the Christian celebration, the central act of the community worship. The eucharist as a sacrament contains everything. We become what we celebrate. The eucharist has many aspects; it is a meal, a sacrifice, a thanksgiving, a covenant, a gift, a presence, and a memorial.

On the night before he died, Jesus "took some bread, and when he had given thanks, broke it and gave it to them saying, 'This is my body which will be given for you; do this in memory of me.' He did the same with the cup after supper, and said, 'This cup is a new covenant in my blood which will be poured out for you'" (Luke 22:19-20).

The eucharist is a memorial of God's saving

love and covenant of fidelity. The memorial is not simply a memory of the past but a dynamic remembering of God leading people to freedom. Such a memory brings comfort to the present and hope for the future. Memories were extremely important for Israel. At the Last Supper, Jesus and the disciples were celebrating a passover meal, recalling the Exodus journey. Such remembering is a *kairos*: a time when time is not measured by a watch (*chronos*, time), but by the sacred moment of God's presence. By remembering the suffering servant of Yahweh (Isaiah 53), the Jewish people gave thanks for the obedient servant of God who gave his life for his people.

A Living Presence

The eucharist speaks to us about presence and expresses the living presence of Jesus in the Christian community. It is interpersonal and transforming rather than static. Jesus wanted to be present to the community, to the church, and to the world. He is Emmanuel, God with us. The resurrected Christ has transcended our reality and invites us through the eucharist to discover new depths in our life.

People in love desire deep communion with each other. Jesus so loves us he longs for this communion with us, and wants to be present with us. "For where two or three meet in my name, I shall be there with them" (Matthew 18:20). The presence of Jesus in the eucharist is not only in the host. Some believe that Jesus becomes present only at the consecration, and that the consecration is the climax of the Mass. But Jesus is first present to us in the liturgy of the Word. At the consecration, the physical appearance of the host does not change, but the meaning does for those who believe. The host does become the body of Christ for the faithful. Jesus is thus present in another way to the community.

The eucharist is also a sacrifice. The whole notion of sacrifice has undergone change. In early Israel, the "material" of a sacrifice was important. However by the time of the exile, the emphasis had shifted to interior dispositions. The sacrifice Jesus offered was his own life, the total giving of himself in love. Eucharist as sacrifice is a *kenosis*, a letting go that allows God to become the core of our being.

After the fourth century, with the rise of a cultic view of the priesthood and the clericalism of ministry, sacrifice was once again perceived as something that was offered by the priest for the people, and the belief that Christ was the unbloody sacrifice offered by the priest developed. Calvary was being re-enacted in an unbloody manner. The concept of sacrifice is often associated with killing and pain, but the Christian understanding of sacrifice is lifegiving and relational. The eucharist is a sacrifice because gifts of life are being exchanged, ours and Christ's, and the Father's love is being poured out on us through the Spirit. The sacrifice of the eucharist is intended to transform us, to call us to say a new "yes" to the Father, as Jesus did in his self-emptying on the cross.

The eucharist is an expression of a new creation where God meets us through the living presence of Jesus. The bread and wine symbolize the ordinary things of creation that are transformed by God's power. The calling down of the Spirit during the eucharistic liturgy is an invitation for the breath of God to fill Earth with the fruits of peace and reconciliation.

The following ideas may be useful in teaching about the eucharist.

Discuss the meaning of "presence" with those you teach. Through personal examples and roleplay, illustrate the various kinds of presence. Suggest examples of physical presence, psychological presence, and spiritual presence. Ask: What inhibits people from being really present to each other? In what ways might the eucharist be regarded as "the presence of Jesus"? How important is the idea of people being present to each other during Mass?

With your students, look for examples of sacrifice in history. Which acts of sacrifice have impressed them? On what occasions have they sacrificed? When have others sacrificed for them? Which saints especially impressed them with their lives as gifts for others? How is the Mass a sacrifice?

Invite students to trace the history of the Mass and how it has been celebrated throughout the history of Christianity.

Have them draw a chart to illustrate the main features of these changes and research the different kinds of gathering places for eucharist celebrations, from household churches to cathedrals in the Middle Ages to basic Christian communities today. Have them design their idea of a church building that is appropriate for a eucharistic celebration.

Together examine the symbols of bread and wine. In what way is the bread of the eucharist a call to respond to the hunger of the world? How might the eucharist be linked with social justice? What does it mean to say the eucharist is "hunger for the world?"

"Eucharist" means thanksgiving. Ask students why the eucharist is a thanksgiving. Have them recall some of the special blessings in their lives and express thanks for them.

Suggest examples of ritual meals from religions of the world and social customs. Research the passover meal of Judaism. Ask: In what ways might the eucharist be considered as a ritual meal?

Jesus is present in the liturgy of the Word. Consider ways in which students listen or don't listen. Have one of them read the following Sunday's gospel and ask all to listen attentively to the words and the message of the passage.

Reconciliation, or Penance

Reconciliation as a sacrament is concerned with the forgiveness of Jesus that brings us to new beginnings. Sin is a breakdown in our relationship with God through the failure to love. Such a breakdown may be expressed in the social sins of an unjust society, of destructive behavior toward people or ourselves, in violence to our environment, or in a failure to be faithful to our responsibilities as disciples of Jesus. God always loves us and invites us to a new creation.

Conversion is the acknowledgement of God in our lives and turning toward God. Conversion is not an act, it is a process of growth and change, of saying "yes" to God who does not easily accept "no" from us.

The history of penance in the church is one of evolution. In the early church, sin was seen as a menace to the life of the Christian community and thus the emphasis on reconciliation was on restoration of what had been broken. The three great sins of murder, apostasy, and adultery struck at the very life of the community, and through a public act of penance the penitent acknowledged guilt. Reconciliation was an ecclesial event in which the whole community was involved.

The excessive rigorism of church practices after the fourth century removed the practice of reconciliation from the lives of most Christians. There was more emphasis on the individual and less on the community. After the seventh century, the Irish missionaries carried to mainland Europe their practice of individual penance, which grew out of a spiritual direction tradition in the monasteries. The stress was on confession and then on "satisfaction" in which the person made up for sins by doing certain good deeds or prayers. To standardize these practices, tariff or penance books were composed. Sins were categorized and graded according to the penance given.

The Irish system became the system of the universal church by the Middle Ages. Confession became a private practice and was administered by clerics. The emphasis on form and matter tended to view the sacrament as a judicial process, with the penitent as a prisoner going before the priest, who acted as judge and passed sentence on the penitent. Private confession became the norm and the ecclesial dimension was virtually non-existent. Basically this situation remained unchanged until Vatican II.

Three rites of penance were introduced after the Council. The first rite is individual penance, the second is a group meeting with opportunities for individual penance, and the third rite is a communal celebration.

The following teaching approaches may assist your group to appreciate and experience reconciliation in their own lives.

Share stories of forgiveness. When is it easy or difficult to forgive others? How may there be a healing of hurts? Reflect on some of the forgiveness stories in the life of Jesus, for example: the woman caught in adultery (John 8:1-11), the woman who was a sinner (Luke 7:37-50), the prodigal son (Luke 15:11-32). The story of the prodigal son contains these key elements of reconciliation: 1) movement away from a relationship with a loving father, 2) alienation of the younger son, 3) insight about the prospect of returning home, 4) return and reconciliation, 5) restoration by the father and celebration, 6) contrasting attitudes of the two sons about the father-son relationship.

Read stories with your class about reconciliation between countries and families. Give examples of how racism is destructive to harmony within a social system or country. How are the God-images of people related to their willingness to experience reconciliation? Ask students to consider the lives of some prominent peacemakers in various countries of the world and also to consider the role of various world agencies who try to achieve reconciliation, for example the United Nations. Using this information, invite your class to prepare a reconciliation service.

Anointing of the Sick
In the letter of James we read:

> If one of you is ill, send for the leaders of the church, and they must anoint you with oil in the name of the Lord and pray over you. The prayer of faith will save you and the Lord will raise you up again; and if you have committed any sins, you will be forgiven (James 5:14-15).

The sacrament of anointing is a sacrament for the sick. Vatican II decided to change the name from "Extreme Unction" to "Anointing of the Sick" to restore the more traditional name and meaning.

In the early church the practice of anointing as described by James was commonplace. The rite was for the sick, and it was done by lay people as well as presbyters. It was intended for the restoration of the body as well as the spirit.

By the Middle Ages, the sacrament changed. Anointing of the sick became linked with the sacrament of penance, and then with its administration at the time of death. Hence it became a sacrament of fear, the last act before death and judgment. The new rite has restored links with the earlier tradition. It stresses community and is to be administered to people with every kind of sickness, including psychological illness.

Sickness is an integral part of being a human person. It is not just a bodily disorder because it affects the whole person. Our present social system removes people from the family in times of serious sickness. They are reduced to a state of complete dependency, and in many cases, family members feel awkward in the presence of the one who is sick. People today also tend to practice denial. They try to distract the sick person from stark reminders of the fragility of life and personal mortality.

Discuss this with students as well as the question of healing. How do they feel about sickness? About healing? How do they heal others? How have others healed them? Invite them to share experiences of sickness, either personal or family stories. Ask them to identify some of the points of pain in our present society. What is being done by individuals and groups to alleviate these social ills? What more could be done?

After this discussion, study the rite of anointing of the sick with students and then invite them to prepare a paraliturgy for healing.

Teaching about Marriage

The sacrament of marriage is somewhat different from the other sacraments. It integrates the whole area of intimacy, relationships, sexuality, and generativity into a theological whole. Rapid changes in our society have raised major pastoral questions about the viability of Christian marriage in the face of an erosion of traditional family values. Negative influences in our society, such as the trivialization of love, reluctance to engage in life commitments, and economic pressures, have placed families under enormous pressure.

Soaring divorce rates give a depressing testimony to the power of these influences. The nuclear family of parents and children is a recent social phenomenon. Traditionally the concept of family meant extended relatives as well as the nuclear family. From an anthropological perspective, marriage is one of the most fundamental institutions.

The church only gradually came to accept marriage as a sacrament. The first Christians married according to civil law and sometimes asked the bishop for his blessing. From the fourth century on, there is evidence of liturgical rites being celebrated for Christian marriages. By the twelfth century, marriage as a sacrament was accepted.

A Positive Theology

For a number of reasons, the church has struggled to evolve a positive theology of marriage. Unlike the other sacraments, which were created by the church from the ministry of Jesus, marriage had always been a basic human institution and therefore the church had to incorporate it into its liturgical practice and pastoral life. It is significant that the ministers of the sacrament of marriage are the man and woman themselves. The teaching church has suffered from a pessimistic view of sexuality and has tended to see the need for a sacrament of marriage as a rescue operation from the "weakness of the flesh." Such attitudes by leadership, which was male and celibate, have cast a long shadow across the inherited biblical theology of covenant.

The bible described marriage as part of the covenant relationship between God, humankind, and Earth. The book of Hosea describes Hosea's search for his straying wife, Gomer, and his fidelity to her in spite of her prostitution. The story of Hosea is likened to the faithfulness of Yahweh who is married to the people of Israel. In the New Testament, marriage is associated with the mystery of Christ who is the focus of all relationships with God and all creation.

Marriage is the sacrament of human friendship. People are made in God's image (Genesis 1:27) and are relational by nature (Genesis 2:18). Marriage expresses the mystery of the Trinity in the giving and receiving of love, a love which is to be shared. The *kenosis* of letting go in love is to allow God's love to be the energy of this relationship.

A Covenant Relationship

In the theology of marriage, there has been a shift from a contract-legal model to a covenant-relationship model. The church continues to grapple with complex pastoral issues such as divorce and remarriage, interfaith marriages, and reconciling the "indissolubility" principle with specific pastoral situations.

The Christian family is meant to be the foundational element of the Christian community. The sacrament of marriage is the public ritual of affirming and celebrating God's love as manifested through the commitment and intimacy of husband and wife to each other.

Consider the following teaching activities.

Have students collect contemporary songs, cartoons, or articles about marriage and love. What are the messages? Do students agree with these messages? What do they learn about love from the media? Invite them to discuss with married couples what marriage means for them. What are ways to enhance the quality of married life?

Ask students to research references to marriage in the bible. Study such passages as Book of Hosea, Mark 10:6-9, the entire Song of Songs, Ephesians 5:21-32, and John 4:7-12.

Ask students to find out about covenant in the bible. In what ways might Christian marriage be described as a covenant relationship? Have them view a film on marriage. What does it tell them about relationships? Finally, have them actually prepare a marriage liturgy.

Some people choose not to marry but to lead a single life. A special form of single life commitment is to become a religious sister, brother, or priest. Invite students to interview some of these people and discuss with them their life of commitment.

Holy Orders, or Ordination

All Christians are by baptism called to participate in the life of the church and the world. Through baptism we receive the gifts of the spirit which empower us to engage in the work of the kingdom of God (1 Corinthians 12). Ministry is service to the community for the sake of the kingdom. One special ministry is the sacrament of ordination, which is an office and charism to lead the Christian community in liturgy and be an animator of ministries. Ordained ministry has to be understood within the context of the diversity of ministries in the Christian community.

The early Christians had a very flexible approach to ministry. However, the eventual need for structures and organization motivated them to establish permanent offices of leadership. By the third century, all Christian communities had bishops, presbyters, and deacons. Many of the primal ministries (e.g., widows, waiters on tables) disappeared or were subsumed under the major ministries. When Christianity became the official religion of the Roman Empire, the style and practice of ministry became closely linked with the Roman civil bureaucracy. Gradually the official church leadership separated from the rest of the Christian community. The dichotomy between clergy and laity was clearly evident by the Middle Ages. The sacrament of sacred orders was the consecration of

chosen people to be bishops, priests, and deacons. During the medieval period the order of deacons became a step toward priestly ordination.

The sacrament of ordination is intended for leading the Christian community to holiness of life by presiding over liturgies, celebrating the sacraments, preaching the Word, and empowering all the people of God to realize and use their various gifts for the welfare of the community. Ordination does not give a priest power for his own sake but for service to others. The Council of Chalcedon (451 C.E.) expressly forbade ordination for a person who was not attached to a community (Canon 6).

Since Vatican II, there has been a return to the primal tradition of ministry. New ministries have evolved to respond to the pastoral aspirations of the people. Priests are rediscovering their roles of working with the laity in a collaborative approach to ministry. According to Paul: "There is a variety of gifts but always the same spirit; there are all sorts of service to be done, but always to the same Lord" (1 Corinthians 12:4-5).

Major Questions about Ministry

Our contemporary church is facing major questions about ministry, among them the role of women in ministry, the validation of orders among Christian churches, clarification of the role of priesthood in relation to other ministries, presiding over the eucharist in communities that have no priest, and formation for future ministry. Belief about ministry reflects our belief about the nature of the church. Post-Vatican II ecclesiology has broadened our appreciation of church as a community of disciples. We are now searching to develop ministries that are appropriate for this ecclesiology.

These teaching activities might help students better understand Holy Orders.

Ask students to interview a priest about his priesthood, and then discuss the meaning of ministry.

Research the evolution of ministry from the early church to our present time. Why is there now such an interest in ministry? Also have students make a list of the various ministries in their parish.

Together find out the name and roles of the ministries mentioned in the New Testament letters and in Acts of the Apostles. As part of this, study the changing roles of women in ministry. Compare the place of women in the ministry of Jesus with the situation today.

If possible, visit a group of religious brothers or sisters with your students. Ask them about their commitment to God in their religious communities and how they view their ministries.

What do your students understand "vocation" to mean? How is vocation related to the ministry of Jesus? Have them examine the gospels to see how the disciples understood their ministries and/or their vocations.

Ask students: Why do you think the exercise of power is such a key dimension of ministry today? Should this change? Why or why not?

Conclusion

Sacraments are celebrations by the Christian community that mark the passages of our human life. Through rituals and symbols, Christians experience God's love embracing our humanity through sacraments. The seven sacraments, however, have to be understood within the context of sacramentality, which celebrates God's presence within the whole of creation. The seven sacraments support and encourage us to encounter God more fully in the mystery of God's revelation through the life of the church.

Ways to Respond

•Invite your class to prepare individual posters or banners for each of the seven sacraments. They can do this in groups or individually, depending on the size of your group. When these are completed, display them in your parish church or hall as a learning experience for everyone in the parish.

•Roleplay the sacrament rites with your class. First review the steps involved in each rite and then assign parts. Have students supply props and take turns being parents, penitents, married couples, ordained ministers, etc. Present these roleplays to other classes or to groups of parents and other parishioners.

Questions for Reflection and/or Discussion

•What do the sacraments mean to you personally? Which sacrament has the greatest influence on your daily life patterns? Why?

•How do your students react to a study of the sacraments? Do they find them a source of life and grace? What could you do to help them find sacrament signs and symbols more meaningful?

•Do you consider yourself a "sacrament" in the broad sense? Why or why not? How are you a sign for others?

•What do you understand sacramentality to mean? How do the seven sacraments contribute to sacramentality?

•In what practical ways might you help your students to relate sacraments and sacramentality to their everyday concerns and decisions?

Notes

Chapter 10

Teaching about Christian Morality

Every day people are making decisions about what to do or not do. There are so many questions about moral behavior. Is this a right action? How should we live? Are the Ten Commandments still a useful moral guide? Is my conscience the ultimate guide for my life? Can the government make laws that contravene a person's religious beliefs?

Morality is concerned with the quality of a person's life and conduct and in choosing courses of action that are appropriate for individuals and society. Christian morality seeks to enhance the dignity of people who are created in the image of God. It expresses a view of human life that has been bequeathed to us by Jesus and shaped by his teachings.

Contemporary Attitudes

The whole area of morality is very complex today. In previous generations, the authority of families and the church was influential in setting moral standards. An explicit and specific moral code was formulated and reinforced by threats of divine retribution for transgressors. Many Christians have vivid memories of fiery sermons on hell as just punishment for those who did not obey the laws of God and the church. Today we recognize the ambivalence of

many moral situations. The ways in which we perceive, value, and behave have been complicated by diverse influences. Categories of moral certitudes have been blurred by our technological society, which has generated many moral dilemmas. Examples of these dilemmas are: Is nuclear war ever permissible? What is a Christian position for genetic engineering? In the face of growing world hunger, are we justified in spending astronomical amounts of money for space research? Is recycling a moral injunction?

Dogmatic moral positions have been challenged by the discoveries about human behavior in the social sciences, especially in the areas of psychology and sociology. Our appreciation of people as social beings leads us to acknowledge the many ambiguities of human experience. We are confronted with a wide array of questions. Should homosexuals be fully incorporated into the Christian community? Is not to smoke a moral imperative? Does a wholistic view of marriage allow couples to make their own choices about contraception? When does life begin in the womb? The problem of accommodation to cultural norms of morality is an acute one. How does the church find its moral path between accommodation and the ideals of the gospel?

The current ideology of individualism postulates that the starting point for moral decisions is the individual's preference, without any reference to the good of the community. The cult of individualism does not accept communal guidelines for moral decisions—from the church or anyone else. The accepted dictum seems to be: If it feels right, do it. Although this brand of individualistic morality is irresponsible, it represents an important shift from the oppression of a tribal morality that did not allow individuals to take responsibility for their actions. Christian people today are asked to assume a greater personal responsibility for their lives.

Christians have become more aware that they need to make personal moral responses according to their consciences, as well as according to the teachings of the church. The church has sought to be faithful to its moral heritage from Jesus in a diversity of cultural and pastoral situations. Over the centuries, it has modified its moral teachings as new insights about the human condition have emerged. In such areas of moral teaching as slavery, usury (the charging of interest rates), suicide, marriage involving non-Catholics, ecology, and the distribution of wealth, the church has undergone significant shifts in its moral consciousness. We can be sure that there will be many more changes as the Christian community enters more deeply into conversations with its culture.

Historical Development

The first Christians inherited a morality that was founded on the Jewish understanding of covenant. The covenant represented the promise of God's provident care, with a reciprocal pledge of fidelity from God's people. Morality was understood as fidelity to the commandments of the covenant. The code of the covenant was the guiding principle of ethics for the Israelites. The Ten Commandments summarized the spirituality of the covenant, which was being in right relationship with God and neighbor. The story of the Jewish people is a story of how they fared in their endeavors to obey the laws of the covenant.

Jesus announced the reign of God as a fulfillment of the covenant and the inauguration of a new covenant. He preached the urgency of *metanoia*, a radical conversion to the way of discipleship. The message of the kingdom was the core of the preaching of Jesus and a kingdom vision demanded a life vision that was open to God's love. This was often in stark contrast with prevailing values in society. The "Jesus principle" of the gospel was the command to love one another. Love is not selective or exclusive. In the last judgment scene as portrayed by Matthew 25:31-46, Jesus situates kingdom morality in the context of service to the most marginalized. To follow Jesus is to be displaced from a position of security to the vulnerable position of being with the outsiders.

Early Christianity struggled to preserve the integrity of the human person against the influence of Gnosticism. Gnosticism exalted the spiritual as against the material. The denigration of the body and sexuality by the Gnostics affected the way Christians approached morality. Redemption was considered fundamentally a "spiritual event," and a faith commitment entailed a rejection of the "world" in the incarnational sense.

Another complicating factor in the shape of Christian morality throughout the ages has been the church-state alliance after the fourth century. The marriage of church and state tended to link morality with a political and religious status quo as distinct from the prophetic witness of Christians to the radical dream of Jesus. The emergence of a monastic and hermitical tradition of spirituality contrasted the superiority of the "flight from world" spirituality with the moral laxity of those who chose to live in a corrupt society. The exaltation of the monastic ideal among religious leaders left many contentious moral issues in day-to-day living without a Christian perspective.

There was no systematic development of moral theology until the sixteenth century. Early Christian writers responded to particular ethical issues as these were encountered by the

Christian community. However, after the sixth century there were a number of developments in moral teaching, and these began to influence the character and direction of Christian morality. When the practice of confession began to spread beyond the shores of Ireland after the eighth century, penance books became associated with perceptions and practices of morality.

Penance books were intended to assist pastors in designating specific acts of reparation for particular sins. They sought to standardize the scope of penances given in confession. However, a consequence of this practice meant that Christian morality became more identified with the sacrament of penance. The widespread use of penance books unwittingly nurtured an attitude of minimalism in Christian morality. People could feel morally justified if they avoided specific sins as listed in the penance books or only committed "little ones." The gospel imperative to be radically open to God's love faded before a minimalist interpretation of the Christian way. Does an attitude of avoiding sin constitute the Christian call? The confession slant in Christian morality tended to emphasize justice rather than God's mercy.

Assigning a penance for particular sins also suggested that sinners were like prisoners going before a judge to receive a sentence for their crimes. This kind of quantifying of God's mercy failed to take into appreciation God's love "as gift," not as a deserved reward. Medieval scholars such as Aquinas and other scholastic theologians systematized and integrated morality within the framework of God's care for creation and our generation in the image of God. Doctrine, scripture, and theology were brought together to express a unified vision of revelation. Compared to later developments in moral theology, the scholastic period closely linked faith and action.

Reformation Times
During the fourteenth century, the "nominalists" taught the uniqueness of each existing thing. Society was bonded by external law and authority. Nominalism contributed to the reduction of the moral code as a series of individual acts with little awareness of social morality. The loss of a sense of social sin opened the way for a morality of individualism. Nominalism also reinforced the view that the source of the moral code was the external authority of the church. The Reformation polarized religious opinions. Bloody religious wars accentuated the movement in the church toward rigid positions. In the struggle to survive, the churches felt that there was little time for theory and finer points of morality. What was needed was clarity in teachings and definitive laws. Concerted action in reform was the order of the day. In such a climate of crisis, authority and law were utilized to bring cohesion to the church's moral teaching.

Code of Canon Law
This was revised in the seventeenth century and was another factor in the growth of legalism. Acts were judged mortal or venial in degrees of seriousness according to detailed criteria for evaluation. Before going to confession, Catholics were taught to categorize their sins according to their degree of gravity. "Tell the big ones first, little ones after!" was a catechetical injunction. Loyalty to the teaching church was a sign of orthodoxy and loyalty meant following the moral code of the church, cost what it may. A prevailing belief was that the church knew better than any individual about moral acts, because the church represented the authority of Christ on earth and individual Christians, through lack of education or sinful blindness, could not discover moral truth.

The Council of Trent (1545-1563) established seminary training for priests in places situated well away from the distractions of the world. The teaching of moral theology in the seminaries tended to focus on behavior rather than gospel values. Such teaching gave precise answers to moral dilemmas posed within a confessional context. As ministers of the sacrament of confession, priests were taught to give correct answers in the confessional and to ensure that sacraments were validly received.

This brief overview of the evolution of moral theology indicates that it gradually became detached from the scriptures and dogmatic theology and became legalistic. When moral theology drifted away from its biblical roots, it became a separate entity directed by canon lawyers. The heresy of Jansenism infected morality with a deeply pessimistic perspective on Christian life. Sin abounded in Jansenist morality. A rigorous standard of conduct was demanded, while grace was limited to a chosen few. In the Jansenist view, hell was overflowing and heaven had few inhabitants. The "justice" of God was a paramount consideration.

The Twentieth Century

During the first half of the twentieth century, Catholic morality was, in the words of Richard McCormick: "confession-orientated, magisterium-dominated, law-related, sin-centered, and seminary-controlled." However, in the latter part of this century, moral theology underwent dramatic shifts in its scope and focus. Contemporary moral theology is characterized by these features:

- It is grounded in biblical studies and the writings of the early church Fathers.
- It is no longer identified with the sacrament of penance but is situated within the life and teachings of Jesus.
- It was an inductive method by attending to concrete life experiences rather than the deductive method of starting with fixed abstract universal principles and applying these principles without regard to history and culture.
- It incorporates the insights of the social sciences so that human behavior and consciousness are appreciated from a wholistic perspective.
- It is placed within a pastoral context. It is not an academic exercise but a discerned reflection on the struggle to be fully human in the light of the gospel and the teaching traditions of the faith community.

- It challenges all economic, social, and religious oppressions. In this century, the church has spoken strongly on a wide range of social issues such as nuclear weapons, the right to work, the dignity of labor, freedom of association, the distribution of wealth, and the environment.

In the latter part of this century there were rising tensions within the church about morality. One basic source of this tension was the difference between a classical and historical understanding of morality. The classical understanding emphasized unchanging norms of natural law that are interpreted by the magisterium of the church. The historical understanding explored morality within the evolution of cultures and sought to expand the moral traditions of the church to include new interpretations of morality. This struggle continues today.

Christian Morality

Jesus said: "I have come that you may have life and have it to the full" (John 10:10). When Jesus was asked by a lawyer: "What must I do to inherit eternal life?" Jesus answered, "What is written in the law? What do you read there?" He replied: "You must love the Lord your God with all your heart, with all your soul, with all your strength, and with all your mind, and your neighbor as yourself." "You have answered right," replied Jesus. "Do this and life is yours" (Luke 10:25-28). These two proclamations by Jesus reflect the heart of Christian morality, that is, to love God and to love one's neighbor as oneself as we search for the fullness of life in Jesus. We are created as daughters and sons of God, called to be responsible stewards in the world. Christ is the way, the truth, and the light. Jesus said: "I am the light of the world. Those who follow me will not be walking in the dark; they will have the light of life" (John 8:12).

In the letter to the Colossians, we read that Christ is "the image of the unseen God, the firstborn of all creation, for in him were created all things in heaven and on earth" (Colossians

1:15-16). It is this Jesus who taught that we must care for the universal neighbor, not just friends and not just likable people. In the Beatitudes (Matthew 5:3-12), he declares "blessed" those who live in utter dependence on God and whose involvement with others is characterized by mercy and reconciliation. The God of Jesus is a loving parent who anxiously waits for wayward children to return home (Luke 15:11-32). The kingdom of God is a unifying symbol of *shalom*, especially for those who are alienated by personal or social sin. Christian morality has its inspiration in the life and teachings of Jesus.

Christians and Law

The issue of the law was a contentious one for Jesus in his dealings with the Pharisees. According to them, people were righteous if they were faithful to the specifications of the law. Jesus taught that we must go beyond the letter of the law and live its spirit (Matthew 5:17ff). He preached that moral actions are a consequence of conversion of heart. The *metanoia* of the kingdom makes us ready to accept the will of God (Mark 2:27; Matthew 23:23). The letters of Paul speak about the new law of the Spirit. Christ is the new law, and when we live a life of love we are set free from the bondage of sin. Paul writes to the Corinthians: "The letter of the law kills, but the Spirit gives life" (2 Corinthians 3:6).

Tension between the law and the spirit of the law is a recurring motif in the story of Christian morality. Many of us can recall times when we followed the letter of the law, but failed to show charity. A friend of mine shared with me her anguish at not being able to attend the funeral of her best friend because the service was in a funeral parlor and not in a church! Christian law should always facilitate the activity of the reign of God. Law is never an end in itself. Church law belongs to the pastoral mission of the church to announce the good news of Jesus. When laws lose this foundational reference point, they become oppressive weapons of power.

Natural Law

There are different kinds of law, for example, natural law, state laws, Christian laws, and church laws. In the history of Christian morality, the concept of natural law has been a major influence in establishing moral norms, especially within the Catholic community. Since the time of Aristotle (384-322 B.C.E.), the concept of a higher law existing beyond human laws has been widely accepted in western philosophy. Throughout history, there have been two basic interpretations of natural law. Cicero (d.43 B.C.E.) and Ulpian (d.228 C.E.) represent the two key positions on natural law.

In Cicero's view, reason has a central place in law and hence law is a product of the social, religious, historical, and psychological dimensions of human life. Such an approach recognizes the historical and evolutionary nature of people and hence the need to reinterpret moral norms according to new insights.

The classical view of morality considers natural law from the perspective of the unchanging order of the universe which was established by God. God's creation formed a certain natural order that was not be tampered with by humankind. Ulpian's idea of natural law is very physical. According to him, laws are discovered by observing human functions in their natural state. Humankind is moral if it is faithful to the God-given laws that govern nature. The classical view is essentially static and concentrates on the biological dimension of the moral act. Classical moral theology begins with abstract principles and deduces moral norms from these unchanging principles.

Contemporary moral theologians are attempting to close the gap between the historical and classical positions by validating moral norms against the reality of what is ultimately good for the individual and society. A revisionist understanding of morality accepts the historical evolutionary nature of humankind. We recognize that what we now do in good faith may not necessarily be ethical in some future era of consciousness. However the "Jesus principle" is always the foundation stone for Christian morality. Hopefully, open conversations between the teaching authority of the bishops, the moral theologians, and the lived experiences of faithful Christians will ensure fidelity to gospel moral imperatives.

Moral Development

Our moral responses are affected by our levels of moral awareness. Researchers in moral development, such as Piaget, Kohlberg, and Fowler, have proposed that people make moral decisions according to the stages they have attained in moral reasoning. Although the theories have been criticized by feminist writers and those who question the lockstep assumptions of the stage theory, it seems that people come to moral acts from different levels of awareness. There appear to be at least four levels of moral awareness.

•*Level 1: The Reward/punishment stage:* "Will I be rewarded or punished if I do this action?"

•*Level 2: Corporate ethic stage:* "I will do this (not do this) because this is what the group (church, family, friends) expects me to do."

•*Level 3: Conflict stage:* "My own integrity says I should do this, but my action will cause pain to others. I feel tension in taking this stand."

•*Level 4: Universal principle stage:* "I am at peace with this act because it is best for our world. I don't really care about the consequences for myself."

Moral decision making is a very complex process. We might make decisions from the stance of level three and then revert back to level one for another moral dilemma. However, in any exploration of Christian morality, we must take into account the fact that people make moral decisions from these various levels of consciousness.

Another factor in moral development is the question of freedom. Freedom is a very tenuous thing. Human freedom is very limited because of our social, religious, psychological, and cultural conditioning. Our environment shapes our values and moral judgments. We have to constantly ask ourselves in what sense we are free to make moral decisions.

Conscience

Conscience is awareness of personal responsibility. It is our inner core leading us toward a right path. A person needs to be self-directive according to values that affirm the dignity of persons created in the image of God. By following our consciences, we make morally responsible decisions according to the ideals of love and compassion. The church has always upheld the primacy of one's conscience provided a person acts for the greatest good of all concerned and takes care to inform his or her conscience. The prime right of conscience does not mean doing what one likes. On the contrary, the common welfare is the test of whether people are responsible by following their conscience. We tend to so easily rationalize what we do. Hence Christians should keep themselves informed about the teachings of the church and attend carefully to Christian mentors. In the Hebrew Scriptures, the word "heart" captures our idea of conscience (e.g., Job 27:6). In the writings of Paul, he links the idea of "heart" to his understanding of conscience as an illumination and judge of our inner selves (Romans 2:15).

Missing the Mark

The derivative of the word sin is "missing the mark," as an arrow misses its target. When we substitute something other than God in our quest for being, we miss the mark, we sin. Sin is an inversion of our baptism. It is alienation from the core of our source of being, which is God.

The bible deals extensively with the problem of sin. In the opening chapters of Genesis, sin is described as a kind of ripple flowing out in circles from a breakdown in relationships with God. The four circles of sin are: 1) alienation from self (Genesis 3:7), 2) destruction to family (Genesis 4:8), 3) a cosmic force of destruction

(Genesis 6:17), and 4) a disintegration of the community (Genesis 11:1-9). A modern trend to do away with sin is a denial of the reality of evil. The ravages of sin are painfully obvious in our world.

All sin involves choice. We are responsible and accountable for our actions. According to the last judgment scene (Matthew 25), our final judgment is a confirmation of a whole series of choices that we have made during a lifetime of relating (or not relating) creatively with the community. In Matthew's description of the final sin (Matthew 25:32ff), it is a failure to respond compassionately to the poor.

Sin is a failure to act lovingly. The historical link between confession and morality emphasized sins of action or commission (e.g., lying, cheating, stealing, hurting). The last judgment description is a somber warning that perhaps the worst sins are ones of omission rather than commission. The privatization of morality has enabled unjust political and economic systems to rule, unchecked by challenges from the church. Our social consciences should be stirring us to resist the power of sinful systems that denigrate human dignity. Micah's injunction for justice is as relevant today as it was eight centuries before Christ: "This is what Yahweh asks of you and only this, to act justly, to love tenderly, and to walk humbly with your God" (Micah 6:8).

Conclusion

The rainbow symbol of the first covenant is our great sign of hope that God's saving power will prevail over evil. Conversion is a process of reorientating our being toward God, the shifting of our horizons. According to theologian Bernard Lonergan, conversion affects all of our conscious and intentional operations. It directs our gaze, pervades our imagination, releases the symbols that penetrate to the depths of our psyche. It enriches our understanding, guides our judgments, and reinforces our decisions. It is a wholehearted commitment to God that influences our entire life. The concept of fundamental option relates to our understanding of conversion. Fundamental option is a basic decision about our life orientation. We are what we choose to be.

Our sins are not stones around our necks but paving stones on the journey toward God. Through reconciliation, we incorporate our failures and sins into the flow of the journey. The very act of sin can be an invitation to redirect our energy toward its divine source. God's love cannot be measured according to our limits of justice.

Christian morality is a choice for life. The life principle is the axis for making moral decisions. When Christians live morally, they make responsible choices to choose life for themselves and the community. Love is the generating and energizing force for life. The core commandment of Jesus is to give oneself in love to nurture life in another. "This is my commandment: love one another as I have loved you" (John 15:12).

Ways to Respond

•From your study of the gospels, make a list of the teachings of Jesus about a moral life. Are these teachings still relevant today?

•Examine some current moral issues and discuss with your students the moral principles and values involved. What is a Christian stance toward issues such as racism, sexism, destruction of the environment, abortion, violence, euthanasia, and job-related strikes?

•Here are some statements about morality. Analyze them with your students from a Christian perspective:

Everyone is doing it, so why can't I?

If nobody gets hurt by this action, then it's okay.

I just follow what the church teaches. That's my moral code.

I make decisions according to my conscience.

Too bad I was born a Christian. It stops me from having lots of fun.

Questions for Reflection and/or Discussion

•What is your personal definition of morality? Where did you get this definition? Are you able to live by it?

•What do your students understand morality to mean? Do they attempt to make moral decisions? On what do they base these decisions?

•How would you define "conscience"? What guidelines would you give those you teach to help them develop a Christian conscience?

•What do you think the term "social sin" means? What examples of social sin are you aware of? What can you do about them?

•Have you ever experienced a conversion in your life? When? What changed in your life as a result of this?

Notes

The Place of Story
in Religious Education

Storytelling is the oldest tradition of communicating God's revelation to us. Whenever we hear "Once upon a time...," we settle back ready to enjoy a story. Stories express us. They link us with one another, explore who we are, and illuminate aspects of the mystery of our being as people.

As a child I loved stories. I would join my four brothers after supper to sit and listen to old Jack Shultz, our German farm worker. Taking his time, Jack would light up his pipe, puff it contentedly, and then, by the flickering kerosene lamp, take us back to the old days with tales about cyclones, snakes, and new settlements. Outside the darkness was complete and the swamps sang with a chorus of night creatures. Inside the farm house, we laughed at the stories, shivered at the near misses with deadly snakes, and tried to imagine those "early days."

I was transported further back into time some years later when I stood at the tombstone of the Trestons near the farm "Cloontreston" near Knock, County Mayo in Ireland. I mused on the journey of my grandfather, almost a hundred years before, who left this place to begin his odyssey across the ocean to the other side of the world in Australia. Family stories, like all stories, communicate something of our

identity and paradoxes. Stories present a window from which to view the world. Through stories, we gather diverse events into a tale of our life that has new insight and meaning.

People Remember Stories

People remember stories long after they have forgotten the abstract word. Recently a participant at a seminar said to me "Kevin, years ago I attended a seminar that you gave. I've forgotten all that was said, can't even remember the topic, but I've never forgotten the story you told about the window. Thanks for the story; it is my story now." Research confirms that we have the capacity to remember stories for a significantly longer time than content that is couched in abstract language. Little wonder that Jesus used stories (or parables) to communicate his teaching. Who can forget the wayward son, the good Samaritan, the lost sheep, invited guests to the wedding, or the treasure in the field? His appeal to our imagination is an invitation to go beyond our stereotypes and rational thinking, our idols and prejudices. His vision of the reign of God helps us to imagine a very different world, one in which people love, accept, and care for one another. Through his parables, Jesus turned things upside down so that we might begin to penetrate the mystery of the kingdom of God. And yet he used ordinary people and things in his stories—like housewives and sheep and coins—so that we might know that God's kingdom is present in our ordinary lives.

When friends gather, they often engage in storytelling. "You'll never guess what happened to me this morning..." or "My friend Pat was driving home from work yesterday and..." Elie Wiesel once wrote that God made us because God loves stories. Stories really do enter into our lives and we are challenged to explore new possibilities in our relationships with God and our world because of them.

Stories Are Communal

Stories are also for the community. One of my favorites is the Aesop tale of a man, boy, and donkey going to market. The man and the boy tried to please everybody and only succeeded in offending everybody. This story is meaningful to me. From it I have derived a guiding principle for my life. It empowers me to follow my own truth even though some people may not like what I am doing. On several occasions in my life, I have had to make difficult decisions that I knew would upset people. I remembered the story of the man, boy, and the donkey in these times of decision.

Stories can be told orally or through dance, music, poetry, film, and art. The current interest in family history, narrative theology, and national history seem to be a cultural response to find roots in an age of rapid transformation. The speed of cultural change has left many people bewildered and angry. Stories of our heritage offer a cornerstone to cope with the future. In times of crisis, people engage in storytelling. Some of our most influential stories of this century have been created out of the turmoil of the two world wars and the Great Depression.

The church has also witnessed an increased interest in storytelling. The Second Vatican Council struggled to reconnect the past with the emergence of new theologies and pastoral directions. The upsurge of interest in the lives of the saints and a return to the life of the first Christians are just two expressions of the yearning of the Christian community to be faithful to its traditions and roots. As we wander through the gallery of saints, we are reassured that we have friends on our pilgrim journey who have been there before us to light our way.

And yet, we constantly need new stories. As we become aware of the serious depletion of Earth's resources, for example, we need to compose a new story for Earth. The story of the last two hundred years has been one of domination and disregard for the fragility of the interconnectedness of our universe. Almost too late, we are coming to realize that unless we learn to appreciate an alternative story, our children will inherit a wasteland. The new story will have to be one of imagination and responsible care.

We are inherently storymakers because we are human beings, made in the image of God. God is Trinity, relational and dynamic in creativity. Creativity expresses itself in love, and faithful love is really a never-ending story. The Trinity of its very nature is the story of a God who is nurturing, mothering, and generating life. Every time we name the Trinity, we tell a story of the unity of the world in a diversity of relational love. Every Christian story ultimately expresses some feature of the dynamic energy of God who is always receiving and giving.

Decline in Storytelling

Unfortunately, during the last three hundred years, storytelling has been replaced by the formulation of dogmas as a way of explaining the Christian faith. The Enlightenment infected the Christian community with intellectualism, which emphasized the head rather than the heart. At the same time fairytales were banished to preschool, although many of them offer profound insights about humankind. Technological and scientific consciousness strengthened the dominance of rational thought and neglected symbols, myth, and imagination.

Today we need to search for creative ways of telling our Christian story with new images and symbols. The struggle against heresies tended to seduce the evangelizing energies of the church into doctrinal formulations and an obsession with orthodoxy. The restoration of the feminine and imagination has the capacity to empower the Christian community to once again be creative in revealing the wonder of God's graciousness in Jesus.

Jesus As Storyteller

John Shea reminds us that the early Christian strategy was to gather the folks, break bread, and tell the stories. The Christian community faithfully followed the example of Jesus who gathered people together, celebrated companionship in the breaking of bread, and told stories or parables. Jesus the storyteller used village anecdotes to teach lessons about the kingdom. His parables were little windows to glimpse the values of his dream for humankind. They are meant to disturb and energize us, and shake us from our lethargy. They challenge us to take stands that are often in conflict with our culture. The Good Samaritan (Luke 10:29-37), for example, symbolizes the unexpected visitations of God on the journey and challenges us to serve others as God serves. The mustard seed (Matthew 13:31-32) suggests possibilities even in the most obscure situations and challenges us to have unswerving faith. By viewing our own lives as parables with opposites to be reconciled, we can relate each parable of Jesus to the seasons of our life journey.

Many stories are concerned with the journey. One of my favorites is an ancient Hasidic tale about a rabbi who follows his dream by traveling from Krakow to Prague in order to discover a hidden treasure. He eventually finds the treasure, not in Prague but in the hearth of his own home. Our real treasure is within us, but we will not uncover it unless we enter the interior journey. Jesus promises the indwelling of the presence when we allow God to be at home within us (John 15:4).

Religious Education and Story

Religious education engages both teacher and students in the story of God in our world. As teachers you can be good storytellers if you draw from the many resources now available to you, the stories of scripture, your own life experiences, and stories in literature, media, music, art, and folklore.

Also, tell stories in a variety of ways, for example, as oral telling, dance, movement, drama and mime, song and music, puppetry, mobiles, banners, audio/visuals, cassettes, reading, and poetry.

Gather resources for stories from magazines, TV, and family histories. Above all, remember stories from your own life, stories of surprise, discovery, pain, celebration, success and failure, and share these with those you teach.

When telling a story: Know the story orally, know the story intimately before you share it, its moods, sequence, and climax. Look directly at your audience as you tell it and invite audience involvement. Use voice intonations, gestures, pauses, and direct speech effectively so that your story will have the maximum impact.

Conclusion

Story is an essential feature of Christian religious education because the task of teachers is to convey the divine story about God's communion with humankind and the world. Religious stories invite us to find meaning in our own experiences in response to God's invitation to love more completely. The creation story of Genesis (Chapters 2-3) make up the paradigm of all stories. Our human story is a movement from harmony to chaos and back again. The seasons of our life can be told in terms of reconciling the paradoxes of life and death. Stories enable us to imagine new horizons. God's imagination created the world. God invites us through story to create new worlds through our own power of imagination. Perhaps more than ever, we need new stories to bring the hope God offers to our world.

Ways to Respond

•Invite students to compose stories on the following themes: loneliness, Easter, journey, escape, beginnings, failure, and Exodus.

•Consider these parables of Jesus and compose stories to illustrate their themes: Luke 14:15-24 (invited guests who made excuses), Luke 8:5-8 (the sower), Luke 11:5-8 (persistent friend), and Matthew 13:24-30 (weeds and wheat).

•Map your own life in some kind of diagram or graph indicating high and low points, turning points, times of special insight, and special encounters with God. Invite those you teach to do the same, and then write or tell brief stories based on one of the events graphed.

•Encourage your students to compose their own modern-day parables to share insights about the kingdom of God. Review some of Jesus' parables with them before they begin writing.

Questions for Reflection and/or Discussion

•Have those in your class remembered a story you told? (Ask them and find out.) Can you remember a story you heard in religion class? What effect has it had on your life?

•Why is it important to use stories in your teaching? How do those you teach react to stories?

•Do you ever think of Christianity as a story? Why or why not?

•Have you ever had a teacher who was an excellent storyteller? What do you remember about this person? Why was he or she impressive?

•Which stories (parables) of Jesus do you most enjoy? What is your favorite parable? How do you share this and other parables with those you teach?

Notes

Chapter 12

Spirituality for Religious Educators

The word spirituality conjures up images of holy people, saints, hermits, priests, and nuns. Many catechists and teachers believe that spirituality is not for ordinary folks like them! During most of the history of the church, spirituality has been associated with a lifestyle that was solitary, celibate, and remote from the sordid business of living in the everyday world. The "flight from world" motif is woven through the tapestry of Christian spirituality.

One of my favorite stories about spirituality is the story of a sad old abbot of a monastery who watched helplessly as his monks became more gloomy and sterile. No young men of the village joined them. The abbot in despair would to go to the woods to weep and pray.

One day, he met a wise rabbi who told him to return to the monastery with a single message for his monks. He whispered the message to the abbot who immediately returned to the monastery and summoned the brothers to a conference. The abbot spoke to the assembled brothers: "I have just one thing to say to you, brothers. The Messiah is among you!" The crusty old monks sat up from their dozing. But the abbot left the room without another word.

The next week, the brothers anxiously awaited the abbot's conference to hear further details about this startling revelation. But the abbot re-

peated the same message: "The Messiah is among you!" From that day forward, the whole atmosphere of the monastery slowly began to change as the monks watched each other carefully to see who might be the Messiah. They rushed to be of service to each other, cared for the sick, waited at the tables, and prayed for each other with fervor. Soon young men from the village were begging to be admitted as novices because they were so impressed by the spirit of love. Today those monks still serve and wait, hoping to discover the Messiah.

God Is Present

This delightful story tells us much about spirituality. In faith we believe that God is present in the whole of the universe and especially in each person we encounter. The phrase "among you" from the story is a universal refrain for spirituality. Jesus is Emmanuel, among us, with us on the journey. We see the face of Jesus mirrored in the unfolding events of our lives. He is always present with us. It is just a question of whether or not we will open the door to invite Jesus in.

The word spirituality is derived from the Latin root *spirare* meaning "to breathe." God breathed on soil to generate life (Genesis 2:7). Our breathing is a chord of resonance with the divine breathing of the creation hymn of the universe. The Spirit is generating life as God mysteriously graces our moments. Jesus speaks of this hidden power of the Spirit: "The wind blows wherever it pleases; you hear its sound, but you cannot tell where it comes from or where it is going. That is how it is with all who are born of the Spirit" (John 3:8).

Marketplace Spirituality

The term "marketplace spirituality" emphasizes that *where we are* in our lives is our place of grace. The daily round of activities, caring for our families, going to work, teaching religion, paying the bills, and sleeping are all invitations to say "yes" to God's presence without the security of seeing God face to face. As with the wind, we observe only the effects of the Spirit. Jesus best fulfilled his vocation by spending most of his time on earth learning the psalms, fixing plows, and repairing houses in a remote little village in Nazareth. In a world that is competitive and puts a high price on the spectacular, the hidden and ordinary life of Jesus the worker is a timely reminder about sanctity through the mundane.

Spirituality Is for Life

Spirituality is a life process, not a series of good deeds. It is a life stance of orienting our being toward God. It is a religious response to the question: What does it mean to live, given the fact that one day I will die? One does not have spirituality one day and none the next. Spirituality is an attitude of the heart and the way in which we attend to God's invitation to love.

Throughout the history of spirituality, dualism has been a constant threat. Dualism separates body and soul and proposes that the body is a kind of shell enclosing the soul, which is God's spirit in us. Dualistic heresies such as Gnosticism and Jansenism denigrated the body, especially sexuality. They viewed spirituality as freeing oneself of the body in order to release the soul to God.

Wholistic spirituality, on the other hand, is founded on the essential integrity of the human person. The goal of spirituality is to bring us into fuller unity with God, others, and Earth. Spirituality, then, is a movement toward wholeness. As we become more attuned to the interrelatedness of all things, we recognize God as the source of love, drawing together all creation in reconciliation. Strangers become our brothers and sisters. Our perception of Earth changes from an object to a partner. The starting point of our spiritual journey is the grace of the present moment. "Bloom where you are planted" is a favorite saying for spirituality.

If spirituality is attentiveness to the presence of the Spirit, then it is also an invitation to action for justice. Christian spirituality cannot simply be a solitary search to save one's soul. All authentic spirituality is relational because it expresses the love of the Trinity. As co-creators with God, we are called to continue the creation of the world through living and sharing the energizing power of love. This kind of love suggests "letting go" so that God and not the ego self is our center. When the ego reigns in us, God does not. When self is triumphant, God is banished to a religious ideology.

Following the example of Jesus in his *kenosis* or self-emptying (Philippians 2:6-7), we allow God to walk in the places of our weakness. The limits of our brokenness are an acknowledgment that we are humbly standing in need of God's gracious mercy. Recent movements in spirituality have retrieved the primal heritage of Christian spirituality as being for all people as disciples of Jesus, rather than for an elite group.

History records an unfortunate split between theology and spirituality. Both were impoverished by this separation. When spirituality lost its firm roots in scripture and theology, it was prone to the exaggerated, magical, and even the bizarre. When theology was separated from spirituality, it tended to become academic and lacked grounding in life experience. Today all people are encouraged to grow spiritually.

For Christian religious educators, the task of nurturing spirituality for themselves and others is imperative. Religious education without spirituality reduces the whole enterprise to a series of academic propositions without a context. Catechists and religion teachers are not simply detached observers, but witnesses to the message. They are participating in the ministry of Jesus: "I must proclaim the good news of the kingdom of God to other towns, too, because that is what I was sent to do" (Luke 4:43).

This ministry of teaching is part of the whole mission of the church to evangelize. Religious educators are in a privileged position because they are communicators and witnesses to a loving God. They can have a great influence on students in this role. Hopefully they will be able to develop their spirituality through their ministry of teaching as well as in their other life circumstances.

Scriptural Models of Spirituality

The scriptures offer us many passages about the movements of spirituality. I have selected four such passages from the gospels. Read each prayerfully and then study the following reflections:

•Luke 1:26-42, The Annunciation

Mary is the symbol of everyone, and she is the first disciple of Jesus. Let us consider the sequence of this story in Luke's Gospel and relate it to our own experience.

There is a time and place when God takes the initiative to be present in our lives. The Lord greets us with affirmation. We may feel nervous when the Lord enters our life because God's presence can be disturbing. We are consoled by the refrain "Do not be afraid." God invites us to be life-giving people. Will we accept the offer to be generative? We often wonder if we can possibly be fruitful as religion teachers because we are aware of our limits. The Spirit will become our energizing force. If we look about us, we see that others have done great things, so we try to respond to God's invitation by saying: "I'm happy to go along with you." When we receive the Spirit, we immedi-

ately set out to share this gift. We go on mission.

•John 4:5-41, The Woman at the Well

This story illustrates how Jesus moves a person from hostility to hospitality. He is tired and thirsty as he sits by Jacob's well. A Samaritan woman approaches. Then there is dialogue, and it moves through a series of stages: Jesus requests a drink, the woman reacts with suspicion, Jesus speaks about a new kind of water, the woman responds from her own experience, Jesus offers a new life water, and the woman begs for this water. Note that the original request has been reversed.

Jesus then challenges her lifestyle, and the woman acknowledges her fragility. She proclaims Jesus as prophet, and then shares this proclamation. She hurries away to share her encounter with the townsfolk who return to the scene. Jesus evangelizes. He stays for two days with the townspeople who profess faith in him. He empowers the community to believe. The woman has been the catalyst in this happening.

Jesus meets a hostile woman, dialogues with her, and transforms her reality to a new depth of insight into God's revelation.

•Mark 2:1-12, Cure of the Paralytic

First there is a barrier: The paralytic and his helpers cannot reach Jesus. They finally gain access to Jesus by coming down through the roof. Jesus heals first the inner pain and guilt. He challenges the leaders to go beyond the boundaries of their logic about God's mercy. The man is set free to walk again and the community celebrate.

In this model of spirituality, we are asked to imagine another approach to God apart from the logical and rational. Sometimes we have to come "through the roof" of our imagination. God's healing is to bring inner peace as well as physical well being. We also have to face criticism and opposition. Jesus will support us when we have to "walk out in front of everyone."

•Luke 24:13-36, The Road to Emmaus

Two disciples are walking along the road, discussing the Jesus event when they meet a stranger. The disciples share their story of the death of a dream and the stranger tells a new story in which failure is a beginning not an end. In the breaking of the bread, their eyes were opened, and the disciples joyously return to Jerusalem to share the new story.

This story is a favorite story for religious educators because it tells of a teacher who encounters two people who have lost heart and given up. The teacher invites the two to tell their story and listens carefully to them. He "hears" their pain and disappointment and reinterprets the story with a new story of salvation where suffering is the doorway to resurrection. The power of the new story is such that the two disciples feel their "hearts burning." The three celebrate by breaking bread together and, like a shaft of light, insight comes to the disciples. They hurry back to Jerusalem as messengers of the good news.

The Spirituality of Jesus

Jesus as teacher, followed a long line of Jewish teachers, the *hakam*, wise man and rabbi. We know little about the early life of Jesus. During a Jewish child's early years, the child's mother was responsible for the first elements of training, including moral training. Mary, the mother of Jesus, was his first teacher. As Jesus grew older, Joseph would have assumed responsibility for his education, especially in religion and trade. Most teaching was conducted by word of mouth. The teacher told the story and asked questions. Children repeated the story and answered the questions. Perhaps Jesus studied in a synagogue grammar school until his thirteenth year, the year of his bar mitzvah. Although formal schools were not common, scholars tell us that village schools were beginning to appear in New Testament times. In chapter two of Luke's Gospel, Jesus is discovered by his distraught parents "sitting among the doctors, listening to them, and asking them questions" (Luke 2:46).

Many Jewish teenagers were sent to a *bet midrash* or synagogue school. These schools had grown up beside the synagogues after the exile. In such schools, the rabbis taught the Torah, the law. The Torah was a way of life to holiness, rather than a series of laws and regulations. Moses was regarded as the author of the Torah. The heart of the Torah is expressed in the central act of daily worship, the recitation of the *shemah*, especially these words from Deuteronomy: "Listen, Israel: Yahweh our God is the one Yahweh. You shall love Yahweh your God with all your heart, with all your soul, with all your strength. Let these words I urge on you today be written on your heart" (Deuteronomy 6:4-6).

The rabbi's task was to study and meditate on the Torah and to communicate the Torah to his disciples by teaching and example. Some rabbis taught in the synagogue schools; others wandered around the countryside with their disciples. In teaching, a rabbi would often select a text from the Torah and develop the implications of the text in light of a current event or problem. This exploration of a text was called *midrash*. Over the years, there evolved different schools of interpretation among the various teachers of the Torah. In the time of Jesus, there were clear differences in the interpretations of the Torah by such groups as the Zealots, Essenes, Sadducees, Pharisees, and the followers of John the Baptist.

Jesus, the Holy Teacher

Jesus seems to have been a disciple of John the Baptist. After John's imprisonment by Herod, Jesus moved to Galilee to announce the impending coming of the kingdom of God (Mark 1:14-15). For the next three years, he traveled up and down Palestine, healing, teaching, and calling people to repentance. Through our reflections on the gospels, we gain many insights into Jesus as teacher. These features of Jesus as teacher can be a model for the spirituality of religious educators.

Jesus taught people in their own environment. He slept at roadsides, taught from boats, sat on the grass. He did not claim special privileges, but was a companion to his friends and shared their simple way of life. The Son of Man had nowhere to lay his head.

Jesus talked with people. He asked questions and invited responses (Luke 14:6). He pleaded with the disciples to soften his terror of death (Matthew 26:37-38).

Healing was integral to Jesus' teaching mission. Good teaching always brings healing with it.

Jesus taught in parables *(mashal)*. He used everyday examples of fishermen, bakers, travelers, and farmers to convey the message of the kingdom. Through stories, Jesus hoped to break through the confines of religious boundaries and bring people to a conversion of imagination.

Jesus took time out of a busy day to pray. He recognized his mission of revealing the face of God (John 14:10).

He appealed to the heart and spirit of the law (Matthew 12:1-8).

For Jesus, teaching was a service. At the last supper, he knelt and washed feet to exhibit the model of service (John 13:1-14).

Jesus spoke with authority (Matthew 7:28).

He enjoyed celebrations. The parables speak of feasts and celebrations for the kingdom (Luke 15:5-6; Luke 15:24).

Jesus taught that time and patience are necessary for the seed to germinate (Mark 4:26).

In his teaching, he took risks. His friendship and associations with ritual outcasts often got him into trouble (John 4:6; Luke 19:1-10).

The Holy Spirit, or paraclete, was companion to Jesus (Luke 4:14).

Jesus gathered a community of disciples to continue his teaching. The disciples included women (Luke 8:1-3).

Although Jesus encountered fierce opposition, his trust in his Father never wavered (Luke 23:46).

The cross and failure were features of his ministry (John 19:36).

The message of Jesus was one of liberation and an invitation to freedom (Luke 4:18).

Our reflections on the ministry of Jesus help us to appreciate his profound spirituality flowing out of his union with the Father and the Spirit. We, too, are called to an intimate union with God in Christ. Paul writes to the Ephesians: "We are God's work of art, created in Christ Jesus to live a good life as from the beginning he had meant us to live it" (Ephesians 2:10). Paul's prayer is for this mystical union to be realized:

> Out of his infinite glory, may God give you the power through his Spirit for your hidden self to grow strong, so that Christ may live in your hearts through faith, and then planted in love, you will, with all the saints, have the strength to grasp the breadth and the length, the height and the depth; until knowing the love of Christ, which is beyond all knowledge, you are filled with the utter fullness of God (Ephesians 3:16-19).

Nurturing Spirituality

Our personalities, social and ethnic environments, images of God, and personal stories all shape the ways in which we express our spirituality. However, if we Christian educators are people who have chosen to reveal God's gracious love, our own lives need to be touched by many loving experiences of family, community, friends, and students. We learn to receive love as well as give it and to appreciate the gift of ourselves through a healthy self-love.

If God is to become more present in the core of our being, we will have to let go of our securities and allow God to work magic in us. Being poor in spirit, we will humbly look to God as our provider and source of strength.

The gospel injunction is to pray continually (Luke 18:1). Throughout each busy day, we will be touched by those fleeting moments of consciousness when we become aware of God's presence. This can happen any time: in routine jobs at the workplace, preparing lessons, gardening, driving the car, picking up children, cooking, listening to music, feeding the baby, stroking the cat. It is important for our prayer life to set aside specific times for prayer and reading the scriptures. Unless we pray regularly, the incessant demands of each day will devour our spiritual energies. For many Christians, liturgical prayer is a significant expression of prayer.

Through Sabbath, we reestablish our priorities and restore harmonious relationships with the *Imago Dei*, the core of our being. Sabbath times empower us to discern what is ultimately real. Spirituality without Sabbath is like a river bed with no water. Soon the earth cracks and the wind blows away the earth. In addition to community worship, our Sabbath may include a stroll around neighboring streets, doing a tai-chi movement, gardening, or reflective reading. The practice of the Sabbath offers us balance in our over-busy lives.

God gave us the gift of imagination, which is an extension of the divine genius of imagination. Our spirituality is enhanced by cultivating the imagination through song, arts, aesthetic environments, dance, and active imagination exercises.

A passion for justice will lead us into awkward involvements. Yet, a sign of contradiction is a hallmark of Christian spirituality. We may not be able to save the world but each of us can open at least one door of freedom.

Conclusion

When we teach religion, God is there in the activity with us. All the ordinary activities that lead to our lessons are signposts pointing to God's presence with us (Revelation 3:21).

Spirituality is happening right now in the present moment, not in some projected fantasy time. The path of spirituality is one of seasons, of traveling along the way. In the words of an ancient Hebrew prayer: "Victory lies, not in reaching the high points of the road, but in making the journey." Maybe a few laughs on the way will help us get there safely.

Ways to Respond

•Write your own definition of spirituality. Is it something you can attain? Why or why not?

•Reflect on the four scripture models offered in this chapter. To which do you feel most drawn? Share one or all of them with those you teach.

•Spend time reflecting on each of the examples of Jesus as teacher described in this chapter. Try to integrate these approaches into your own teaching.

Questions for Reflection and/or Discussion

•Why do you think most of us consider spirituality "unattainable"? Where did we get this attitude?

•What do those you teach think about spirituality and/or holiness? Do they believe that God is present, always with them? Do you believe this?

•What features of Jesus as teacher most appeal to you? Are any of these already part of your teaching?

•Is prayer a regular part of your life? Do you pray as part of your lesson preparation? Do you pray often with and for your classes?

Notes

Suggested Resources

General

Bargar, Lucie W. 1981 *The Religious Education of Pre-School Children.* Birmingham, AL: Religious Education Press.

Caltagirone, Carmen L. 1982 *The Catechist as Minister.* New York: Alba House.

Cully, Iris V., and Cully, Kendig Brubaker, eds. 1990 *Encyclopedia of Religious Education.* San Francisco: Harper & Row.

Dues, Greg. 1988 *Teaching Religion with Confidence and Joy.* Mystic, CT: Twenty-Third Publications.

Dunne, J.S. 1967 *A Search for God in Time and Memory.* New York: Macmillan.

Dunning, James B. 1993 *Echoing God's Word: Formation for Catechists and Homilists in a Catechumenal Church.* Arlington, VA: The North American Forum on the Catechumenate.

Gietzen, Jean Jeffrey. 1991 *Questions and Answers for Catechists.* Mystic, CT: Twenty-Third Publications.

Groome, Thomas. 1980 *Christian Religious Education: Sharing Our Story and Vision.* San Francisco: Harper & Row.

_____. 1991 *Sharing Faith.* Harper-SanFrancisco.

Harris, Maria. 1987 *Teaching and Religious Imagination.* San Francisco: Harper & Row.

_____. 1989 *Fashion Me A People: Curriculum and the Church.* Philadelphia: Westminster/John Knox Press.

Hill, Brennan. 1988 *Key Dimensions of Religious Education.* Winona, MN: St. Mary's Press.

Jungmann, J.A. 1962 *The Good News: Yesterday and Today.* New York: Sadlier.

McCarty, Jim. 1990 *The Confident Catechist.* Dubuque: Brown-ROA.

Manternach, Janaan, and Pfeifer, Carl. 1991 *Creative Catechist: A Comprehensive, Illustrated Guide for Religion Teachers.* Mystic, CT: Twenty-Third Publications.

Martin, Thomas M. 1988 *What Should I Teach?* New York: Paulist Press.

Moran, Gabriel. 1981 *Interplay: A Theory of Religion and Education.* Winona, MN: St. Mary's Press.

_____. 1983 *Religious Education Development,* Minneapolis: Winston Press.

O'Neal, Debbie. 1992 *More Than Glue and Glitter: A Classroom Guide for Volunteer Teachers.* Minneapolis: Augsburg Books.

Ratcliff, Donald, ed., 1992 *Handbook of Children's Religious Education.* Birmingham, AL: Religious Education Press.

_____. 1988 *Handbook of Preschool Religious Education.* Birmingham, AL: Religious Education Press.

Schippe, Cullen. 1990 *Planting, Watering, Growing! The Volunteer Catechist's*

Companion. Granada Hills, CA: Sandalprints Publishing.

Schultz, Joani. 1986 *Youth Ministry Cargo.* Loveland, Colorado: Group Books, Inc.

Sisters of Notre Dame. 1985 *Saints and Feast Days.* Chicago: Loyola University Press.

Sorensen, David A., and Sorensen, Barbara Degrote. 1992 *Kindling the Spark: A Dialog with Christian Teachers on Their Work.* Chicago: ACTA.

Tighe, Jeanne, and Szentkeresti, Karen. 1986 *Rethinking Adult Religious Education.* New York: Paulist Press.

Turner, V. 1968 *The Ritual Process.* Chicago: Aldine Press.

Walsh, Michael, ed. 1991 *Butler's Lives of the Saints, concise edition.* San Francisco: HarperSanFrancisco.

Walters, Thomas P. 1986 *Making a Difference: A Catechist's Guide to Successful Classroom Management.* Kansas City: Sheed & Ward.

Warren, Michael, ed. 1983 *Source Book for Modern Catechetics.* Winona, MN: St. Mary's Press.

_____. 1989 *Faith, Culture and the Worshipping Community.* New York: Paulist Press.

Bible

Glavich, Kathleen, S.N.D. 1989 *Leading Students into Scripture.* Mystic, CT: Twenty-Third Publications.

McFarlan, Donald. 1986 *Concise Bible Dictionary.* Mystic, CT: Twenty-Third Publications.

Lee, B.J. 1988 *The Galilean Jewishness of Jesus.* New York: Paulist Press.

Link, Mark. 1987 *Path Through Scripture.* Allen, TX: Tabor Publishing.

McBrien, Philip. 1992 *How to Teach with the Lectionary.* Mystic, CT: Twenty-Third Publications.

Riley, William. 1986 *The Tale of Two Testaments.* Mystic, CT: Twenty-Third Publications.

Church

Altemose, Charlene, M.S.C. 1989 *Why Do Catholics...?: A Guide to Catholic Belief and Practice.* Dubuque: Brown-ROA.

Bausch, William. 1981 *Pilgrim Church: A Popular History of Catholic Christianity.* Mystic, CT: Twenty-Third Publications.

Cunningham, L.S. 1985 *The Catholic Heritage.* New York: Crossroad.

Doyle, Dennis M. 1992 *The Church Emerging From Vatican II: A Popular Approach to Contemporary Catholicism.* Mystic, CT: Twenty-Third Publications.

Dulles, Avery. 1974 *Models of the Church.* New York: Doubleday.

Marthaler, Berard L. 1992 *The Creed* (revised). Mystic, CT: Twenty-Third Publications.

Pasco, Rowanne and Redford, John. 1991 *Faith Alive: A New Presentation of Catholic Belief and Practice.* Mystic, CT: Twenty-Third Publications.

Creation Theology

Berry, Thomas. 1991 *Befriending the Earth: A Theology of Reconciliation Between Humans and the Earth.* Mystic, CT: Twenty-Third Publications.

Carroll, D. 1987 *Toward a Story of the Earth: Essays in the Theology of Creation.* Dublin: Dominican Publications.

Dowd, Michael. 1991 *Earthspirit: A Handbook for Nurturing an Ecological Spirituality.* Mystic, CT: Twenty-Third Publications.

Fox, Matthew. 1983 *Original Blessing.* Santa Fe: Bear & Company.

Kenny, J. and Miller, R., eds. 1987 *Fireball and the Lotus: Emerging Spirituality from Ancient Roots.* Santa Fe: Bear & Company.

Morality

Harigan, J.P. 1986 *As I Have Loved You: The Challenge of Christian Ethics.* New York: Paulist Press.

McBride, Alfred, O.Praem. 1990 *The Ten Commandments: Sounds of Love from Sinai.* Cincinnati: St. Anthony Messenger Press.

Scott, Sharon. 1985 *Peer Pressure Reversal: An Adult Guide to Developing a Responsible Child.* Amherst, MA: Human Resource Development Press, Inc.

Westley, Dick. 1984 *Morality and Its Beyond.* Mystic, CT: Twenty-Third Publications.

Prayer

Brokamp, Marilyn, O.S.F. 1987 *Prayer Times for Intermediate Grades.* Cincinnati: St. Anthony Messenger Press.

_____. 1987 *Prayer Times for Primary Grades.* Cincinnati: St. Anthony Messenger Press.

Costello, Gwen. 1990 *Prayer Services for Religious Educators.* Mystic, CT: Twenty-Third Publications.

_____. 1991 *Praying with Children: 28 Prayer Services for a Variety of Occasions.* Mystic, CT: Twenty-Third Publications.

Cunningham, Lawrence S. 1989 *Catholic Prayer.* New York: Crossroad.

Donze, Mary Terese, A.S.C., 1982 *In My Heart Room: 16 Love Prayers for Little Children.* Liguori, MO: Liguori Publications.

_____. 1990 *In My Heart Room, Book Two: More Love Prayers for Children.* Liguori, MO: Liguori Publications.

Dues, Greg. 1991 *Seasonal Prayer Services for Teenagers.* Mystic, CT: Twenty-Third Publications.

_____. 1993 *Searching for Faith: Prayer Experiences for Teen Assemblies and Retreats.* Mystic, CT: Twenty-Third Publications.

Glavich, Kathleen, S.N.D. 1993 *Leading Students into Prayer: Ideas and Suggestions from A to Z.* Mystic, CT: Twenty-Third Publications.

Huebsch, William. 1991 *A New Look at Prayer: Searching for Bliss.* Mystic, CT: Twenty-Third Publications.

Jeep, Elizabeth McMahon. 1991 *Children's Daily Prayer.* Chicago: Liturgy Training Publications. This is an annual volume.

Link, Mark. 1988 *Challenge, Decision, Journey: Three Book Prayer Program.* Allen, TX: Tabor Publishing.

Manternach, Janaan and Pfeifer, Carl J. 1989 *And the Children Pray.* Notre Dame, IN: Ave Maria Press.

Reehorst, Jane, B.V.M. 1986, 1991, 1992 *Guided Meditations for Children: How to Teach Children to Pray Using Scriptures.* Volumes 1 (intermediate), 2 (primary), 3 (high school). Dubuque: W.C. Brown.

Rinker, Rosalind. 1992 *Learning Conversational Prayer.* Collegeville, MN: The Liturgical Press.

Roberto, John. 1992 *Family Rituals and Celebrations.* New Rochelle, NY: Don Bosco Multimedia.

Sacraments and Sacramentality

Bausch, William. 1983 *A New Look at the Sacraments.* Mystic, CT: Twenty-Third Publications.

Brown, Kathy and Sokol, Frank C., eds. 1989 *Issues in the Christian Initiation of Children: Catechesis and Liturgy.* Chicago: Liturgy Training Publications.

Browning, Robert L. and Reed, Roy. 1985 *The Sacraments in Religious Education and Liturgy.* Birmingham, AL: Religious Education Press.

Costello, Gwen. 1992 *Reconciliation Services for Children.* Mystic, CT: Twenty-Third Publications.

_____. 1993 *Maria's First Communion* Mystic, CT: Twenty-Third Publications.

_____. 1993 *Ricky's First Reconciliation* Mystic, CT: Twenty-Third Publications.

Duggan, Robert D., and Maureen Kelly. 1992 *The Christian Initiation of Children: Hope for the Future.* New York: Paulist Press.

Huebsch, William. 1990 *Rethinking Sacraments: Holy Moments in Daily Living.* Mystic, CT: Twenty-Third Publications.

Martos, Joseph. 1981 *Doors to the Sacred.* New York: Triumph Books.

Mick, Lawrence E. 1987 *Understanding the Sacraments Today.* Collegeville, MN: The Liturgical Press.

Smith, P. 1987 *Teaching Sacraments.* Wilmington, DE: Michael Glazier.

Spirituality

Brennan, P.J. 1985 *Spirituality for an Anxious Age.* Chicago: Thomas More Press.

Broccolo, Gerard. 1990 *Vital Spiritualities: Naming the Holy in Your Life.* Notre Dame, IN: Ave Maria Press.

Coles, Robert. 1990 *The Spiritual Life of Children.* Boston: Houghton Mifflin Company.

DeMello, Anthony. 1978 *Sadhana: A Way to God.* New York: Doubleday, Image Books.

Palmer, Parker J. 1983 *To Know As We Are Known: A Spirituality of Education.* San Francisco: Harper & Row.

Puls, Joan, 1993 *Seek Treasures in Small Fields: Everyday Holiness.* Mystic, CT: Twenty-Third Publications.

Treston, Kevin. 1988 *Paths and Stories: Spirituality for Teachers.* Brisbane, Australia: Creation Enterprises.

Storytelling

Bausch, William. 1984 *Storytelling: Imagination and Faith.* Mystic, CT: Twenty-Third Publications.

DeMello, Anthony. 1988 *Song of the Bird.* New York: Doubleday.

Estrada, C.L. 1987 *Telling Stories Like Jesus Did.* San Jose, CA: Resource Publications.

van Bemmel, John G. 1991 *Take Heart, Catechist: Twenty Stories for Guidance and Growth.* Mystic, CT: Twenty-Third Publications.

Of Related Interest...

CREATIVE CATECHIST
Janaan Manternach & Carl J. Pfeifer

An overview of the meaning, the history and the goal of catechesis. Keys to being creative and how to use tools to communicate God's Word. In-depth resource guide included.
ISBN: 0-89622-490-2, 160 pp, $9.95

**HOW TO TEACH
WITH THE LECTIONARY**
Philip J. McBrien

A comprehensive step toward effectively employing lectionary-based catechesis. Catechists in conversation interpret biblical texts and plan lessons. Leader's guide also available.
ISBN: 0-89622-522-4, 176 pp, $9.95

TAKE HEART, CATECHIST
Twenty Stories for Guidance & Growth
John Van Bemmel

Relevant stories to boost morale and stimulate thought. Includes a helpful subject finder.
ISBN: 0-89622-459-7, 104 pp, $5.95

**TEACHING RELIGION WITH
CONFIDENCE AND JOY**
Greg Dues

A solid blending of practical, tested ideas and sensitive reflections on the importance of religious education.
ISBN: 0-89622-359-0, 80 pp, $4.95

XXIII

Available at religious bookstores or from

**TWENTY-THIRD
PUBLICATIONS**
P.O. Box 180
Mystic, CT 06355

1-800-321-0411